Markus, Planter of Trees

A Memoir

Markus, Planter of Trees

By Elizabeth Meyer Liener

iUniverse, Inc.
Bloomington

Markus, Planter of Trees
A Memoir

iUniverse books may be ordered through booksellers or by contacting:

iUniverse
1663 Liberty Drive
Bloomington, IN 47403
www.iuniverse.com
1-800-Authors (1-800-288-4677)

Because of the dynamic nature of the Internet, any web addresses or links contained in this book may have changed since publication and may no longer be valid. The views expressed in this work are solely those of the author and do not necessarily reflect the views of the publisher, and the publisher hereby disclaims any responsibility for them.

Any people depicted in stock imagery provided by Thinkstock are models, and such images are being used for illustrative purposes only.

Certain stock imagery © Thinkstock.

ISBN: 978-1-4759-4629-1 (sc)
ISBN: 978-1-4759-4628-4 (hc)
ISBN: 978-1-4759-4627-7 (e)

Library of Congress Control Number: 2012915986

Printed in the United States of America

iUniverse rev. date: 11/29/2012

He will be like a tree planted near water, which spreads out its roots along a brook and does not see when heat comes, whose foliage is ever fresh; it will not worry in a year of drought and will not stop producing fruit.

Jeremiah 17:8

Contents

Preface

*M*y paternal grandfather was involved in helping Marcus Rosenberg and his brother, David, move their fledgling business in a positive direction. My parents have been friends with David and Gussie Rosenberg since the late 1950s. Nonetheless, I never once had a conversation with Marcus Rosenberg. I had heard about him. I was aware of some of his accomplishments. But I had very little knowledge of who he was as a person.

In doing my research for this book, I spoke with more than one hundred people who knew Marcus Rosenberg—family, friends, employees, business colleagues, and those with whom he worked in the Jewish community. Through these interviews, I came to understand in many ways who Marcus Rosenberg was as a man, a business owner, and a builder of community. Through these interviews, his exceptional story of survival and perseverance came together.

Marcus Rosenberg was a Holocaust survivor, but the experience of those tumultuous and horrifying years neither bound nor restricted his ability to dream, work, and accomplish. He was a man of integrity, a complex individual who possessed a brilliant mind and a relentless tenacity to achieve what he believed was important. After finding his way to the United States, Marcus Rosenberg worked earnestly and tirelessly to build an exceptionally successful business. He applied that same resolve and determination to his work in the community, bringing to Dallas, Texas, aspects of Judaism not present there before. Marcus Rosenberg enabled a sustained commitment to Jewish education in the city. The institutions he built were foundations for Orthodox Judaism and Jewish life in general. His generosity touched countless people in the Dallas community and around the world. The trees he planted bore beautiful fruit, not for himself to enjoy, but for others. His efforts were meaningful and lasting.

For those of us who have enjoyed and continue to enjoy the fruits of his labor, and for those who are yet to come, Marcus Rosenberg's daring and courageous story—one filled with numerous twists and turns and near brushes with death—should be known and understood. We can then more fully appreciate all that this resolute man accomplished in the face of daunting obstacles in order to serve those in his and future generations.

I would like to thank Ann Rosenberg for giving me the opportunity to undertake this project. I am honored to share the story of her beloved husband.

Abraham Markus Rosenberg
Avraham Mordechai ben Yekutiel Yehuda
November 6, 1923–February 18, 2005

Z"L
May his memory be a blessing.

Part One

❧

The Old Country

Chapter One

The wind howled mercilessly outside, banging a loose shutter against the window frame over and over. With a start, Markus Rosenberg sat up in his bed. Seeing the time on his clock, he was careful not to awaken his three brothers, who were still sleeping soundly in their beds. Manny and David needed to get up too but not yet. They'd be savoring the warmth of their thick down-filled blankets a little longer before venturing outside into the cold, dark Czechoslovakian winter morning. Little Aaron, not yet three years old, slept peacefully alongside his brothers, his long curls framing his gentle face. Still too young for *cheder*, the young boy did not need to rise with his brothers, who would be immersed in Jewish studies by six a.m.

Markus was so excited by the upcoming day's learning that he could hardly sleep through the night. Bava Basra was filled with *mishnayos* that fascinated him. He never tired of the myriad business laws and ethics spanning volumes of *gemara*. The rationales and arguments of the various rabbinic scholars throughout the ages engaged him, captivated him. He must be at the cheder the minute the rebbe opened the door for the students and not a moment later.

Before getting out of bed, Markus closed his eyes and whispered the words of the Modeh Ani:

I gratefully thank You, O living and eternal King, for You have returned my soul within me with compassion—abundant is Your faithfulness.

Finishing the *netilas yadayim*, or ritual washing of the hands, Markus quietly recited the Hebrew words:

The beginning of wisdom is the fear of Hashem—good understanding to all their practitioners; His praise endures forever. Blessed is the Name of His glorious kingdom for all eternity.

After quickly dressing, Markus ran to the kitchen to pack some bread and butter in a sack. It was just past five forty, and he could hear Manny and David moving about upstairs.

Markus paused for a moment, thinking about his youngest brother. In just a few months, Aaron would have an *upsherin*, and his beautiful long curls would be snipped away, leaving the sidelocks, *peyos*, like the ones Markus had. Aaron would then begin wearing a *kippa* and going to cheder with the other boys his age.

But Aaron wouldn't walk to cheder alone like his big brothers. The *behelfer*, the rabbi's assistant at the cheder, would come by the houses to pick up the very young children. In the winter especially, it was too cold and too dark for these little ones to go out at that hour without an adult. Care had to be taken when walking on the snowy streets alongside the horses and buggies.

Once safely delivered to the cheder, the three- and four-year old boys would begin learning the *aleph-beis*. By the time Aaron would turn six, he would start his Chumash studies. And when he reached that milestone, he'd have a *tzumazal chumash*, a small *kiddush* celebration in his family's home on Shabbos after morning services at shul. The neighbors would come, along with the rabbi, to listen to Aaron recite what he'd learned from the weekly *parasha*. Afterward, the well-wishers would congratulate the young boy and enjoy the delicious *lekash*, or sweet honey cake, that Aaron's mother would bake for the occasion. Manny, Markus, and David each had had their turns at these new beginnings; not long from now, it would be Aaron's turn as well.

Another huge gust of wind whisked Markus out of his passing thoughts and back into the current moment. Grabbing his coat, he ran out the front door into the frigid January darkness.

The Rosenbergs lived in Bardejov, Czechoslovakia; their home, located on Radničné námestie, the town square, was steps away from the Saint Egidius Basilica, an impressive centuries-old Roman Catholic church that dominated the still-sleeping square. Markus spotted his two closest friends, Avraham (Avrum) Leiser Grussgott and Abish (Bandi) Rosenwaser, trudging up from behind the church. Once they joined Markus, the three boys travelled as quickly as they could to the cheder. When they arrived, the rebbe, Melamed Rab Abish, was just opening the door. Markus wished his teacher a good morning.

Bardejov Town Square

⁓⁓*⁓*⁓*⁓*⁓*⁓*⁓*

Jarred from a deep sleep, Anna Tannenbaum Rosenberg jumped up when she heard the front door slam. She glanced at the clock; no time to waste. Today was Wednesday, market day, and the stalls would soon be filled with people—buyers and sellers, townsfolk and peasants. Chickens and eggs, potatoes, cabbage, and onions would again be teeming over the wooden bins of the marketplace.

Anna had much to do at home before leaving for market. Soon, Hancha would be waking up to help Anna begin the day. Hancha, a peasant woman from the Slovak countryside, lived with the Rosenbergs during the week and returned to her own family on the weekends. On weekdays, Hancha helped with chores—getting wood from the shed, drawing water, laundering clothes and linens, taking care of the children. She'd been a faithful employee of the bustling family for many years.

Anna looked out the frosty window of her bedroom, took a deep breath, and for a moment, thought about the day ahead.

She knew her three oldest boys were off learning Torah. Their sister Erika was a few streets away, living in her aunts' home. Rather than sharing a bedroom with her four brothers, she felt more comfortable under the roof of her three favorite aunts. Erika would be waking up soon to help them open their grocery store, and then she would be off to school.

Before feeding young Aaron breakfast, Anna would prepare supper for the family. She would also get sandwiches ready for the boys to pick up on their way from cheder to state school. While Hancha helped with almost every aspect of running the Rosenberg home, she did not do any cooking. Because of the

Anna Tannenbaum Rosenberg

stringencies of *kashrus* and because Hancha wasn't Jewish, Anna had full command of food preparation. Once supper was prepared, Anna would run out the door to work. Anna was always running, never walking. The competition was stiff, and being the salesperson of the family, Anna knew that she needed to be the very first one at the doors of the retail grocers where she did business.

The Rosenbergs owned a wholesale grocery operation located in a small corner market down the street from their home. Anna went out and sold to the retailers in the town, peddling her sugar, flour, eggs, margarine, spices, soap, and even candies that the Rosenbergs packaged themselves. She was the dealmaker for the retailers. Her husband, Solomon, was the dealmaker when it came to buying supplies. He visited the farmers and the mills, with his young sons in tow so they could learn the trade. Solomon ordered their supplies by the carload and stored them in a warehouse. The Rosenbergs then sold their products by the bag, by the bushel, and by the case to retailers—both Jewish and non-Jewish. Solomon, Anna, and their boys tended to the store as well, working together to carve out a living and a life for themselves.

While Solomon Rosenberg was a native of Bardejov, Anna was not. Anna Tannenbaum Rosenberg was born in Nowy Sacz, in the Galicia region of Poland. She was one of eight children—two boys and six girls. When Anna was young, her family moved to Prague, where she was educated and spent her formative years. Around 1918, when her two brothers, Oscar and Bernard (Bernie), came close to the age when they would be conscripted into the army, their parents sent them off to Wilkes-Barre, Pennsylvania, to live with Anna's aunt and uncle, Tillie and Sam Lenovitz. Oscar and Bernie joined their four cousins—Max, David, Bernie, and Sydney—and together, they all worked in the Lenovitz family grocery store. The spelling of the Tannenbaum brothers' last name was changed to *Tanenbaum* upon entry into the United States.

As the two boys grew older, they each moved to Texas; Bernie settled in Austin, while Oscar went to Greenville. Though he did not have *s'micha*, Bernie initially went to Austin to fill a rabbinical position at the local Orthodox shul. In order to better support his growing family, he later switched professions, moving into the liquor business. Oscar found his niche selling dry goods in Greenville.

When it came time for Anna to marry and start a family, she was introduced to Solomon, son of Rabbi Yaakov Rosenberg, a religious teacher at a small yeshiva in Bardejov.

After Anna and Solomon wed, they set up their home in Bardejov. Over the next fifteen years, five children would be born to Anna and Solomon. Their first child, Emanuel (Manny), came into the world in 1921. Markus was next, two years later in 1923. David followed in 1925. Erika, the only daughter, was born in 1927. The last child, Aaron, broke the two-year pattern, making his arrival six years after Erika in 1934.

Rabbi Yaakov Rosenberg

By 1936, some eight thousand people called Bardejov their home. In this small, scenic town nestled in the foothills of the Carpathian Mountains, nearly half of the townspeople were Jewish. The great majority of those Jews were followers of the Sanz dynasty, a Hasidic line founded in the 1800s by Rabbi Chaim Halberstam of Nowy Sacz, Poland. Rabbi Halberstam was known as the Divrei Chaim, named after his great written work on Jewish law. He had seven sons and seven daughters, who had fanned out across the region to begin their own families and expand their sphere of religious influence in various Jewish communities.

Rabbi Naftoli Hirsch Ungar, a great-grandson of the Divrei Chaim, was considered the "Rav" of Bardejov. He lived in a small apartment in the same building as the Rosenberg family. The Rosenberg family's home was upstairs, while the Ungar family's was downstairs. Rav Ungar was very prominent in the Jewish community and held a *minyan* in his apartment, where the Rosenbergs usually *davened* on Shabbos.

⁻⁻*⁻*⁻*⁻*⁻*⁻*⁻*

Following World War I, life in Czechoslovakia was especially pleasant for Jews. After engaging in years of intense diplomatic efforts that spanned the globe, Tomáš Masaryk became the first president of an independent Czechoslovakia in 1918. An enlightened philosopher and politician, Masaryk was instrumental in carving out an independent country for the Czechs and Slovaks who had previously been living under the rule of the Austro-Hungarian Empire. Masaryk respected the religious and economic rights of all citizens, including minorities, and ruled his new democratic country practically and ethically.

Jewish, Catholic, and Protestant children were all allowed to go to school together. In fact, in the northeastern portion of the country where Bardejov was located, all children were required to go to state school. Private schools were not permitted, nor were parochial schools for any of the religions represented in Czechoslovakia. Twice a week, a leader from each of the religious communities taught religious studies in the state schools. Catholic children were instructed by a priest. The other Christians—Lutherans and Greek Orthodox—were taught by clergy from their communities. The Jews learned from a rabbi. At the state school Markus attended, Rabbi Shmuel Grussgott, the father of Markus's best friend, Avrum, taught Jewish history, a bit of gemara, and some Jewish law.

During this time, Czechoslovakian Jews were protected by the government from anti-Semitism. Life was so good and so free under Masaryk's rule that the country was given the nickname, "Little America." However, in 1933, Tomáš Masaryk expressed grave concern to his political inner circle when the national socialist (NAZI) party and a young Adolf Hitler ascended to power in Germany.

Masaryk held office until December 1935, when he resigned due to poor health. In 1937, the country's great leader died on Rosh Hashana. That year, the Jewish New Year was very sad for the Jews of Czechoslovakia, many of whom later attended Masaryk's funeral in Prague. Edvard Beneš took over the leadership of Czechoslovakia.

Meanwhile, Nazi-sponsored book burnings were commonplace throughout Germany, and the Nuremberg laws were already in effect against all Jews living under the rule of the Third Reich.

Chapter Two

$\mathcal{A}$s the boys entered the cheder, they removed their hats, gloves, and coats. Shaking off the frigid cold that had penetrated their heavy winter clothing, the students prepared for the day's learning and morning prayers. Those boys who had already reached *Bar Mitzvah* age began the process of putting on their *tefillin*.

Markus reached for his tefillin bag, carefully taking out the small black leather boxes with their long straps. After rolling up his shirt sleeve and saying the first of several *brachos* related to this ritual, he placed one of the boxes at the top of his left arm and then meticulously wrapped the straps down and around his arm seven times. He fitted the second tefillin's round leather strap around his head, ensuring that the box was centered correctly and the straps weren't twisted. He finished by wrapping the first tefillin's straps around his left hand's fingers in the prescribed manner while reciting, "I will betroth you to Me forever, and I will betroth you to Me with righteousness, justice, kindness, and mercy. I will betroth you to Me with fidelity, and you shall know Hashem." Markus had become a bar mitzvah only six weeks earlier, but he was already an expert at laying tefillin.

The boys all faced the *mizrach*, and morning davening began. As he settled into his prayers, the familiar words enveloped Markus like a parent's warm embrace.

May my prayer to you, Hashem, be at an opportune time; O God, in Your abundant kindness, answer me with the truth of Your salvation.

~~*~*~*~*~*~*

Melamed Rab Abish was seated at the head of a long wooden table. Ten students sat along each side. Each boy had his gemara opened to the page that the class had been studying the previous day. The room was still, and all eyes were on the rabbi as he began to speak quietly.

"Students, we have spent time studying the mishnayos that lay the foundation for Jewish law in the matter of competition in business. Today, I want us to take the next step by beginning to talk about the practical application of these laws." Rab Abish paused for a moment and then continued, "Let us start by exploring some specific questions. For example, can a person open a new business that sells the same product as an existing business? Is someone allowed to go into direct competition with another person who is already established in a particular locale? What are your initial thoughts?"

Markus's friend, Avrum, quickly raised his hand.

"Yes, Avrum," the rabbi said.

"Excuse me, Rab Abish, but it doesn't seem fair that a person should be able to do this. If he does, then he is quite possibly taking away another person's livelihood, is he not?"

Before the rabbi could respond, Markus raised his hand.

"Yes, Markus," the rabbi said.

"Well, I'm not sure if I agree with or, even more importantly, if Jewish law agrees with what Avrum just said. I've been looking over this tractate at home, and if you go to chapter two of Bava Basra, you'll see that the whole chapter is about a dispute between the sages and Rav Yose. The sages say that, in general, the responsibility for preventing damage to a neighbor's property or enterprise lies with the one who is causing the damage."

Markus continued, "On the other hand, Rav Yose holds that one is generally allowed to use his own property as he pleases. In his view, it is up to the threatened party to make sure his property or enterprise is not damaged, with the exception of when the damage to a neighbor results directly from an activity performed within one's property."

With a hint of a smile, the rabbi agreed: "Yes, Markus, you are quite right. The entire discussion of this chapter centers around the conflict that you have identified for us. Let us turn to page 21b."

The boys all turned to the referenced page and waited to hear what Rab Abish would tell them next.

"Here we see that Rav Yehudah says, 'A storekeeper may not distribute parched kernels or walnuts to children, for by doing so, he accustoms them to come to him and thereby deprives other storekeepers of the children's patronage.' So it seems that our sages agree with our friend Avrum's position, does it not?"

"Yes, well, perhaps it seems that way," Markus interjected, "but, Rab Abish, if you look just a little further down, you can see that, despite what Rav Yehudah is proposing above, the sages permit this practice of giving out treats. We know this because, later on, they reason that the storekeeper distributing sweets can say to the other storekeeper, 'I am giving out walnuts; you give out almonds!' That is to say, in the case where both stores are already established, each is permitted to engage in activities that attract customers from the rival store."

"Yes, you are correct, Markus," responded the rabbi.

"But, Rabbi, these passages speak about two stores that are already established. What about when only one store is established and another person wants to set up a competing shop down the road?" asked Avrum.

"Well, Avrum," the rabbi said, "the gemara goes on to say that where a merchant already had a business in a courtyard and a rival came later, even the sages possibly concede that the first merchant can say to the newcomer, 'You are cutting off my livelihood,' and stop him from using the courtyard."

Avrum straightened up on his stool and nodded quickly, clearly pleased with what the rabbi had just read.

"But, Rab Abish," countered Markus, "just after that, it says that this previous ruling is challenged. 'They challenged the ruling from the following *baraisa*: A person may open a rival store next to the store of his fellow or a rival bathhouse next to the bathhouse of his fellow—and the established operator cannot prevent him from doing so because the rival can say to the established operator, "You do as you wish inside your property; I do as I wish inside my property." This baraisa states clearly that, contrary to the previous view, an established merchant cannot prevent the opening of a rival store."

"Of course, what you're saying is true, Markus," the rabbi said, "but if we go a little further, we can see that the gemara says that the previous ruling is not refuted by this baraisa, because there is an alternative view that does not take this position. It was taught in a different baraisa that residents of a *mavoi* can compel one another not to allow the residence among them of a tailor, tanner, teacher, or any other type of craftsman. Specifically, someone who has established a business in a mavoi can prevent the other mavoi residents from renting their property to someone from elsewhere who wishes to ply the same trade. However, it does go on to say that he cannot force his neighbor to refrain from opening a competing business in the mavoi. But Rabban Shimon Ben Gamliel refutes this idea by saying 'He can force even his neighbor to refrain from opening a competing business in the mavoi.'"

Rab Abish stopped reading, glancing at Markus and then at Avrum.

Avrum appeared exasperated.

"The rabbis are giving circular, contradictory answers; this one says that, that one says this," he protested. "What difference does it make if it's a neighbor or an outsider from another village or town? What's fair is fair, and what's not is not."

Markus looked at Rab Abish. "May I continue?" he asked.

Rab Abish nodded.

The other boys around the table listened intently as Markus forged ahead with his arguments, and Rab Abish followed with counter-arguments. For the remainder of the class, they sifted through the various thoughts, views, and rationales of the Talmudic sages on the topics of outsiders versus neighbors, townspeople versus travelling peddlers, salesmen of cosmetics versus salesmen of other products, and so on.

Avrum seemed as if he would fall off his stool at any moment.

"Please Rab Abish," he implored, "Please let us know the answer. Does Halacha permit this type of competition in business or not?"

At that exact moment, Rab Abish smiled and said, "Students, we'll have to continue our studies when you come back after school today. It's seven thirty now; time to go."

The students jumped up from where they sat, and the classroom filled with a cacophony of stools scraping loudly across the floor, gemaras and other religious books hurriedly being put back on bookshelves, and boys gathering their belongings.

The rebbe stopped Markus as he was about to run out the door.

"Markus," the rebbe said softly, "you've had a sharp mind for gemara ever since you started your studies. I see in you a very keen interest in business law and a natural talent for understanding the intricacies of these rulings. You did a very fine job in class today."

Taken aback by the rabbi's generous praise, Markus quickly thanked his rebbe and then dashed out into the cold.

Bardejov cheder boys circa 1936

From left to right: Efraim Neugroshel, unidentified, Mendel Lowy, Elimelech Neugroshel, Avrom Weissberg, Mordechai Yitzchok Weissberg, Pchele Weissberg Courtesy of Bardejov Jewish Preservation Committee, Abraham Grussgott Collection (published in Grussgott, Avrum.1998. *Bardejov Remembered: A Memorial to the Jewish Community of Bardejov, Czechoslovakia 1734-1945*. Brooklyn, NY.)

⌐⌐*⌐*⌐*⌐*⌐*⌐*⌐*

The children had to be at the state school by seven fifty-five, so Markus moved quickly. If a student wasn't there by that time, he'd be forced to wait outside the classroom door until the teacher let him in at the end of the first hour of teaching. A different subject was taught every hour, followed by a five-minute break, which was when the latecomers would be brought into class. Markus had never been one of those students who had to stand outside the door, waiting for the teacher to grant permission to enter, and today was going to be no exception.

On his way to school, Markus ran by his home to grab a sandwich. Once inside the classroom, he settled into his desk which was alphabetically arranged among the desks of the other children whose last names began with *R*.

Markus's classmates and teachers in the Bardejov state school
Markus is standing toward the top left, underneath the handwritten arrow.

The bell rang, and Markus's teacher, Adam Ribar, entered the room. Ribar was an engaging teacher and, for many years, a favorite among the students at the school. Because of his quick mind and genuine curiosity, Markus was a favorite student of Ribar's. Markus and Ribar had frequent discussions during breaks and sometimes even after school, when time allowed. Mainly, the two spoke about history—the history of empires, especially European, and the stories about people who effected change in history. These were the topics that intrigued Markus the most. One person that Markus found particularly captivating was the former Czechoslovakian president, Tomáš Masaryk. And the episode in Masaryk's life that most impressed Markus was his involvement in the Hilsner Affair.

Leopold Hilsner was a Jew living in the village of Polna in Bohemia at the very end of the nineteenth century. Hilsner was a twenty-three-year-old vagrant and a man of low intelligence. In 1899, he was accused of brutally murdering Anežka Hrůzová, a nineteen-year-old Czech Catholic girl who lived in a nearby village. The murder took place in the Brezina Woods on Ash Wednesday. That year, Easter fell on Pesach, and rumors of Jewish blood libel and ritual murder were rampant in the area. Although others were suspected, the investigation concentrated on Hilsner, who ultimately was sentenced to death, even though the evidence was inconsistent and lacking.

Both during the investigation and after the trial, riots against Jews broke out in numerous cities and towns in Bohemia and Moravia. It was in this tense atmosphere that Masaryk, who was a professor of sociology at the Czech University in Prague at that time, intervened forcefully in the case, urging a full review and retrial. Masaryk's courageous stand was not only for Hilsner's justice but also to prove that the superstition of ritual murder was a lie.

Masaryk's stand was not popular with those in power at the time, but for Markus Rosenberg, this story exemplified the fine character of the president and demonstrated to the world that Masaryk and his Czechoslovakia stood for justice and freedom for all people.

~~*~*~*~*~*~*~*

Most of Bardejov's Jews were Hasidic, but in the early part of the twentieth century, men did not generally sit and learn Torah all day. By the age of eighteen or nineteen, nearly all young men worked, either in their parents' businesses or in trades they had been taught.

Bardejov market in the town square
Courtesy of Emil A. Fish.

Solomon Rosenberg's sons Markus and David were a big help to their father and mother. From working with wholesale grocery products from an early age, the two brothers learned all aspects of the business. Frequently, Solomon would take his boys along to the mills when he went to purchase flour and other products. In those mills, Markus's and David's skills for negotiating and deal-making were honed. There they learned the lessons of buying high-quality product at the best possible prices. Experience taught them that there was no going back once the deal was sealed. In those Czechoslovakian mills, Markus and David became well-versed in the art of buying and selling commodities.

The Rosenbergs were regular buyers from several mills, but one mill in particular, managed by a Slovak man, Jozef Drobnak, served the family business well. A good, trusting business relationship that endured for many years was forged between Drobnak and the Rosenbergs.

Markus was exceptionally responsible for his age; so much so that his parents gave him the keys to the cash box for safekeeping. Markus took ownership of watching and handling the money, determining when it should be handed out and when it should not. He was very comfortable being in charge, and his parents were grateful for his initiative and resourcefulness.

Manny did not have an interest in the family grocery business. For him, being confined by four walls was torturous. In his free time, Manny longed to be outdoors doing physical labor. When he finished his compulsory years of schooling and graduated from eighth grade, Manny wanted to further his studies in the state gymnasium (high school). His father, however, was not interested in Manny continuing with secular studies; rather, he wanted him to work in the family grocery business full-time. Manny wouldn't hear of it and told his father that, if he could not go to school, he wanted to go into the lumber business. Solomon finally acquiesced to his eldest son's wishes and found him an apprenticeship with a German Jew in town. Riding his bike or walking the nine miles to the lumberyard and back every day, Manny developed skills and proficiency in the lumber industry.

Like her brothers David and Markus, Erika was also interested and involved in the grocery business. But instead of working in her parents' wholesale company, Erika worked with her three aunts in their retail grocery shop just a few streets away from her family's home. Berta, Hanna, and Sarah Rosenberg were all sisters of Erika's father. The three women lived together in a house with the shop in the front and the

Erika Rosenberg

19

Berta Rosenberg circa 1924

living quarters in the back. Because Erika's mother was rarely home due to her rigorous work schedule, arrangements were made so that Erika would spend her days, and eventually her nights, with her aunts. The doting relatives showered attention on their young niece, and Erika loved being with them. The three women were successful in their business, well-liked, and respected in the community, by both Jews and non-Jews.

Jewish children in Bardejov went to religious school every day. The boys attended cheder both before and after state school as well as on the weekends. The girls went to religious school after regular school and attended *Beis Yaakov* on Saturdays and Sundays.

Though their schedules were very busy with work and schooling, Jewish children also had opportunities to socialize. In Bardejov, the Mizrachi Zionist religious movement became a strong force. The Rosenberg children belonged to Mizrachi and went to meetings to learn about the history of the Jewish homeland and sing Zionist songs. Manny, David, and Erika greatly enjoyed those get-togethers, but

Sarah Rosenberg

because boys and girls mixed and socialized there, Markus never attended, no matter how much his siblings tried to persuade him. Markus instead went to meetings for the Orthodox movement, Agudas Yisroel. With its all-male membership, this youth group focused on traditional Jewish education and culture. In this setting, Markus was comfortable, engaging in additional Torah study and singing in the choir.

During these times, life was good for the Rosenberg family.

The town of Bardejov

Chapter Three

$\mathcal{F}$rances Tanenbaum was filled with such anticipation that she could hardly fall asleep. Tomorrow, she would begin a long journey with her parents, Oscar and Rose Tanenbaum. The trip had been planned for months and would take them from Greenville, Texas, to various spots in Europe to visit several relatives, including her maternal grandparents, whom she and her father had never met. The three Tanenbaums were to stay in Europe from January through March. By the time Frances would turn ten years old, in June of 1938, they would be back in Texas, and Frances could celebrate her birthday with friends from home.

Though she had never been to Europe before, Frances knew the intended route well. Once she and her family arrived in New York, they would depart on a ship bound for Cherbourg, France. Crossing the Atlantic Ocean would take a week. When they arrived, the three would travel to Paris to visit some of her father's cousins. Then they would travel across Germany into Czechoslovakia. After spending time there, they'd move on to Poland to visit her mother's parents.

Frances had cousins in Czechoslovakia in a small town named Bardejov. She couldn't wait to meet one cousin in particular, a girl her age named Erika. Frances knew her father was looking forward to being in Bardejov as well—her father and Erika's mother were brother and sister, and though they had corresponded with one another, they had not seen each other for nearly twenty years.

The prospect of going to these faraway places was thrilling to Frances but somewhat frightening as well. Frances had seen newsreels at the movie theater in Greenville; they showed events and happenings in Europe. Frances saw video clips of the adoring German crowds and the masses of Nazi soldiers marching, their hands outstretched as they passed their revered leader, their *Führer*. Frances had heard her father talking in a hushed voice on the phone with her Uncle Bernie in Austin. She understood from those serious conversations that disturbing things were happening to the Jewish people in Germany. At the age of nine, she didn't realize the full enormity of the situation, but her father and uncle did.

Starting in 1933, the German government had begun implementing a number of anti-Jewish laws that restricted the rights of Jews to be German citizens, to attain an education, and to earn a living. By 1935, the Nuremberg Laws formally stripped German Jews of their citizenship and forbade the marriage of Jews to non-Jewish Germans. Along with Jews around the world, Oscar and Bernie saw dark and ominous signs in what was taking place in Germany and were extremely concerned that the same fate might extend to Jews in other European countries.

Frances and her parents travelled by train through Europe. One night, she was awakened as the train came to a sharp stop at the depot of a small German town. Glancing out the window of her berth, Frances saw several Nazi soldiers walking by outside, their shiny black leather boots glistening in the bright lights of the train station. The silver swastikas on their uniform lapels caught her eye, and she instinctively reached for the necklace she wore, quickly tucking it into her sweater. She didn't want anyone, especially the uniformed men outside, to notice her Star of David. Even though she was an American citizen and the soldiers did not see her, she sensed the danger just outside her train car window.

A couple of weeks later, Frances was in the idyllic town of Bardejov. There were no more Nazis outside her window, just a picturesque European village with beautiful snow-filled streets and new relatives to meet.

Although her cousin Erika did not speak English and Frances did not speak Slovak or Yiddish, they immediately took a liking to each other and greatly enjoyed spending time together. One evening, the two girls were playing with dolls quietly in the living room. Frances heard her father talking to Erika's parents in the next room, but they were speaking in Yiddish, and she could not understand what they were saying. Only years later would Frances learn what was discussed in that conversation.

* ~ * ~ * ~ * ~ * ~ * ~ * ~ * ~ *

Oscar leaned in closely and, in a low voice, said, "Solomon, Anna, you must understand what is happening. We see the news. We hear about it at home, and we read about it in the newspapers. The situation in Germany is bad, really bad. Surely you know that Jews are no longer allowed to be citizens there. They can't hold jobs in the government or in other professions. They can't use the state schools anymore. There are so many restrictions on them, and they are being blamed for all the ills of the country. We are worried sick for you and the children. Won't you please come to the States with us?"

Anna Tannenbaum Rosenberg

Oscar's eyes and his sister's locked for a moment, but then she looked down.

Solomon responded quietly but resolutely, "We know that things are happening in Germany, but surely it can't go on like this forever. The civilized world won't tolerate it for long. The situation will get better. It has to."

Oscar leaned in even closer to his sister and his brother-in-law, pleading, "Solomon, I beg you to please take a realistic look at what is going on. The situation is not getting better; it is getting worse. Much worse. How can you say otherwise?"

Solomon maintained his resolve.

"The German people are civilized. Surely they will not allow these Nazis, these brutes, to stay in power very long. And then everything will go back to normal, the way that it was before."

"How can you say that, Solomon? Maybe you haven't seen the same newsreels I have, but when I watch these clips, I see a nation fully behind their leadership, a nation in love with their leader. The people of Germany support the Nazis. They *are* the Nazis."

Solomon paused for a moment, taking a sip of tea as he continued working through his rationale.

"Well, maybe so. Maybe so, Oscar. I do not know. Time will tell. But that is Germany. It is different here in Czechoslovakia. We live in a democracy. We are free. Jews have protections. And besides, what's in America for us? There's no Jewish life, nothing like what we have here in Bardejov. We appreciate your concern, Oscar, really, but this will blow over. We are observant Jews. We live by the Torah. The Almighty will watch over us. We will be fine."

Oscar sat back and slumped in his chair. Stymied and unable to think of any other words or arguments that might sway his sister and his brother-in-law to see the situation as he did, Oscar reluctantly dropped the discussion for the time being. But he wasn't about to give up. His concern was great, and as he continued to follow the news coming out of Europe, his worries grew even deeper.

Upon his return to Texas, Oscar began working feverishly to bring his family out of Europe before any harm could come to them. He filed paperwork showing he would be financially responsible for his relatives when they came to America. He declared that he would be their sponsor, and that they would have a place to live. He took all the steps needed, but despite Oscar's valiant efforts, the United States had very strict quotas on the number of European immigrants allowed into the country at that time. The visas needed for the Rosenbergs to emigrate from Europe were not granted.

Chapter Four

 ounded in the early 1900s by Andrej Hlinka, a Catholic priest, the Slovak People's Party was a right-wing Slovak political party characterized as strongly Catholic, anti-Atheism, anti-Protestant, anti-Jewish, anti-Communist, and staunchly conservative in nature. During the period of Masaryk's rule of Czechoslovakia, the party was very disappointed that the Slovaks were not given more autonomy. In 1938, when Andrej Hlinka died, the party leadership was taken over by Jozef Tiso, who was also a Catholic priest.

In October 1938, because of British Prime Minister Neville Chamberlain's approach of appeasing Adolf Hitler, Germany annexed the Sudentenland, the German part of Czechoslovakia. As a result, Czechoslovakian President Edvard Beneš fled the country. Political chaos ensued, and the Slovaks declared autonomy, with Tiso as their premier. At that time, the Slovak People's Party joined forces with other nationalist parties and set up the Hlinka's Slovak People's Party/Party of Slovak National Unity.

Several months later in March 1939, Hitler invited Tiso to Berlin to declare the independence of Slovakia and offer German protection to Tiso's new country. If Tiso did not accept this offer, Hitler said he would allow other surrounding countries to annex the Slovakian territories. Tiso took the proposition to the Slovak parliament, which unanimously declared the independence of Slovakia.

The new Slovakia comfortably aligned itself with Nazi policy on handling Jews. In April 1939, Slovakia declared a definition of who was Jewish. Under Tiso's leadership, a new Židovský Kodex (Jewish Code) was adopted in September 1941. This code contained more than 250 anti-Jewish paragraphs that brought into existence laws that, among other things, precluded Jews from owning real estate or luxury goods, excluded Jews from jobs in the public sector, disallowed Jews from participating in sports or cultural events, prohibited Jews from attending secondary schools and universities, and required Jews to wear the Star of David in public. Marriages between Jews and non-Jews were prohibited. Jews were restricted to travelling only in third-class railway cars and were no longer permitted to drive motorcars.

With these new laws on the books, the Aryanization (or nationalization) of Jewish businesses and the confiscation of Jewish property began being carried out throughout Slovakia. In addition, the government began sending Jews to forced labor camps spread around the country.

* ~ * ~ * ~ * ~ * ~ * ~ * ~ * ~ *

Through these volatile and unsettling times, Markus managed to finish the formerly required eight grades of schooling. After that, along with the other Jewish children in Slovakia, he was no longer allowed to attend state school. He and David began working full-time in their parents' grocery business. Manny, who was eighteen years old at the time, wasn't content to sit there and ride out the storm like the rest of his family. During many heated conversations, Manny told his father that he believed the events that were taking place would spell the end of the Jewish population in Europe.

"No, Manny, I don't believe what you're saying. It cannot be. We are good Jews, loyal to the Torah. The Almighty will take care of us," Solomon said each time Manny tried to convince him of the impending dangers.

This frustrated Manny immensely. He had no patience to wait, so he moved to Michalovce in southeastern Slovakia to join Mizrachi, a Jewish Zionist organization. He worked there in a furniture factory while preparing to eventually immigrate to Palestine. Manny's father visited several times to convince him to come home, but Manny's reply was always the same: "No, Father, it's time to go to Palestine."

When the furniture factory ran out of work, Manny moved again, this time to Poprad in central Slovakia, where he engaged in heavy labor on a farm, loading and unloading wagons filled with wet molasses for brewing. He was there until 1940, around the time the British White Paper was issued. This edict effectively closed down legal immigration of Jews into Palestine.

Solomon again went to try to convince his son to come back to Bardejov. Manny refused and instead joined the Slovak army. The army was still enlisting Jewish men, though the Jews were not allowed to fight. Instead of guns, the young Jewish men were issued shovels and picks and did manual labor at military work camps. They were called "Robotnik Zid" or "work Jews." The Jews wore distinctive uniforms to differentiate them from the rest of the soldiers.

Because of his experience in the lumber business, Manny was assigned the job of designing cases for ammunition and grenades and for transporting rifles. He also spent time in the army digging drainable canals.

~~*~*~*~*~*~*~*

During the rule of Masaryk, a large majority of businesses in Czechoslovakia were owned and run by Jews. In Bardejov, the percentage of Jewish-owned businesses was over 90 percent. That changed very quickly between 1939 and 1940 when these enterprises became nationalized. The Rosenbergs' wholesale grocery business was turned over to a Slovak trustee who was none other than Jozef Drobnak, the flour supplier the Rosenbergs had done business with for years. Some of the Aryan trustees who took over Slovakian Jewish businesses immediately removed the former Jewish owners from the operation.

But this was not the case with Drobnak. He understood that he did not have the skills to successfully run the company, so he kept the Rosenbergs in his employ to manage the day-to-day affairs. Arrangements were made between the two parties so that Drobnak would receive a certain percentage of the profits and the Rosenbergs would keep the remainder.

Despite the growing hardships and an overall shortage of food and supplies all over Europe, the Rosenbergs did make a profit. Knowing how to find the commodities their customers wanted, the family had plenty of supplies on hand; so much so that when the German soldiers on duty in Poland ran low on flour or other goods, they would sometimes cross the border into Slovakia and buy what they needed from the Rosenbergs.

⁓⁓*⁓*⁓*⁓*⁓*⁓*⁓*

One evening in late March 1942, Solomon, Markus, and David were closing down the shop for the day. With Pesach just around the corner, a tremendous amount of work needed to be done. Markus was sweeping up while Solomon and David finished unloading a new shipment of sugar.

Unexpectedly, the front door burst open loudly, startling the three Rosenberg men inside. Their eyes immediately shot to the entryway, as they looked to see who or what was at the threshold. Standing in the doorframe was Drobnak, red-faced and visibly upset. Markus and David stared at him as he walked directly toward their father. Shaky and sweating, Drobnak motioned for Solomon to join him in the back room.

Once they were inside the small storeroom, Solomon asked, with great concern, "Jozef, what is wrong? What has happened?"

"Solomon, you need to hide your sons," Drobnak whispered hoarsely. "Right now. They must be out of sight. They can't be seen in the store and not on the street either. They can't be seen anywhere." Drobnak caught his breath and continued, "Your holiday of Passover is coming soon. Just after the religious dinners are over, the Hlinka Garda will be rounding up all the young Jewish men and women over the age of sixteen and sending them to a labor camp in the east. If your sons are in that transport, it is likely you will never see them again."

Solomon's face went white. He couldn't move. He couldn't breathe. Terrible thoughts raced through his head as he asked himself, *Why is this*

29

happening? What will we do? But after a few moments, as he looked up and saw Drobnak, his thoughts refocused.

Solomon knew that Drobnak had no obligation whatsoever to help Markus and David. In fact, he was endangering his own welfare by sharing this information. After all, Drobnak was a member of the Hlinka party. When he recognized the gravity of the situation and the decency in what his colleague had done, Solomon grasped Drobnak's arms and thanked him over and over again, his words of gratitude spilling out and becoming entangled in the hot tears streaming down his face.

Later that night, Solomon and his wife sat down with Markus and David to make the necessary plans.

Chapter Five

❦

$\mathcal{S}$lovakia was the first Axis partner of Germany to agree to the deportation of Jews within the framework of the Final Solution. Tiso and his government embraced the notion of expelling its Jewish population; so much so that the Slovak government offered five hundred German reichsmark to the Nazis for every deported Jew. The deal came with two stipulations: first, Germany would make no claim to the abandoned Jewish property; second, Germany promised that these Jews would never return to Slovakia.

The first roundup in March 1942 was to deliver twenty thousand "young, strong Jews" to

Deportation commission
Gift of Abraham L. Grussgott,
Museum of Jewish Heritage, NY

the Nazi state. A large group of these young people would be tasked with the ominous job of constructing the concentration camp that would bear the name Auschwitz. On the second day of *chol hamoed* Pesach 1942, young Jewish men and women throughout Slovakia began to be aggressively rounded up by the Hlinka Garda, the Slovak equivalent to the Nazi SS. City after city, town after town saw young people taken away, forcibly crowded onto train cattle cars and sent to a destination unknown to them. Jewish families throughout the country were stricken with grief and grave concern for the future.

Markus and David were not among the young people deported that day or the days that followed. For several weeks, the two Rosenberg sons hid in the cellar of their apartment building. While the basement had only one small window through which the sun could shine, having it exposed could give away the boys' whereabouts. All openings to the cellar were covered up to protect the occupants; loose bricks were stacked over the outside window and a large bookcase placed in front of the basement door inside the building.

Markus and David were not alone downstairs. A small group of young people—some of them neighbors, some of them family—were also hiding in the darkness. Through various means, each person there had heard about the roundup in advance and managed to hide before the deportations began. Every day during this period, Anna cooked for those sheltered in the basement, and Erika, too young at the time to be deported, took the food downstairs.

After a few weeks, when the townspeople felt certain the deportations were finally over, Markus, David, and the others emerged from their secret hideout. The rest of their contemporaries from Bardejov—those who had not managed to hide—were gone, never to be seen again.

~~*~*~*~*~*~*~*

Heinrich Himmler, a leading figure in the Nazi party, was quite pleased with the transfer of these young people and worked with Tiso's government to deport the remaining Jews in Slovakia as quickly as possible. Rumors of future deportations spread rapidly across the country and sent the Jewish communities into further panic. Some Jews fled to Hungary, a neighboring country not yet drawn into the war. Others hid in the surrounding woods, hoping to wait out this perilous period. A few Jews attempted to obtain special certificates of exemption that would allow them to avoid deportation. These special certificates were few in number and granted only to those Jews deemed essential to the country's economy.

Markus understood that something ominous was brewing for Slovakian Jewry. Weighing his family's situation carefully, he tried to figure out what realistic options they had for dealing with the impending dangers. Jews could not obtain visas to leave the country legally at that point, so going to America, where Markus's uncles were tirelessly working to bring them out of Europe, was not an alternative. And while the Rosenbergs could attempt to flee illegally into Hungary, that would be a dangerous venture, especially with no family or friends waiting for them on the other side of the border. Crossing over into Poland, where the Rosenbergs did have relatives, was not realistic because that country was under Nazi control. Realizing that they were, for all practical purposes, boxed in, Markus decided to focus his energies on the certificate of exemption.

The Rosenberg family's wholesale grocery ranked third in size among the three wholesale grocers in Bardejov. Being the smallest operation certainly did not bode well for the family's chances for securing an exemption. But Markus knew that his former teacher, Adam Ribar, had become a member of the Hlinka party. Furthermore, Markus had recently heard that Ribar was involved in determining which Jewish businessmen in town would receive the coveted exemptions. Though it appeared to be a long-shot, Markus decided to do whatever he could to become a recipient of this exemption certificate, the piece of paper that would spare him and his family from deportation.

Concerned that he didn't have much time, Markus went to Ribar right away to see what could be done. When Markus arrived, Ribar warmly welcomed his favored student. During their conversation, he confirmed that indeed the decision as to who would receive the special exemptions was being made that very night. Ribar went on to tell Markus that he would do his best to lobby on behalf of the Rosenbergs, despite their ranking behind the other local wholesale grocers. Though Markus was extremely anxious about the situation and afraid for his family's welfare, he took comfort in the sincerity of Ribar's words.

Sensing Markus's angst, Ribar wrote out a special permit that would allow him to be outdoors after the six p.m. curfew imposed on Slovakian Jews. This way, rather than having to wait until the next day, Markus could meet Ribar that night to hear about the decision on the certificate. He was told to come to Ribar's home at midnight.

The hours after their morning meeting dragged by very slowly for Markus. After he checked his watch repeatedly throughout the day, at last the time came for him to go to Ribar's home. When he arrived just before midnight, he saw that the lights were out and assumed his former teacher had not yet returned from the Hlinka meeting. With the Star of David prominently displayed on his sweater, Markus chose to wait across the street in a darkened store doorway in order not to arouse suspicion. Despite the curfew waiver Ribar had given him, Markus wasn't looking for trouble from any Hlinka Garda who might happen by. Thirty minutes passed and then an hour. Markus continued to wait in the shadows, chilled by the night air. Finally, around one thirty a.m., Ribar returned home. Markus stepped out of the doorway and crossed the street.

Motioning him over, Ribar said, "Markus, I am so glad you are here. I was worried you might leave since my meeting ran longer than expected."

With anticipation in his voice, Markus said, "Thank you again for giving me the permit so I could see you tonight."

"Markus, I know it's late, so I will be brief. It took a lot of work and a lot of talking on my part, but somehow I did manage to convince the other officials tonight that your family should receive the special exemption. Honestly, I am not completely sure how it happened, but it did. So you can be assured that the Rosenberg family will be able to stay in Bardejov now and will continue to be the wholesale grocery supplier for the town."

Markus's eyes grew soft, and as he reached over to grasp his teacher's arm, he said quietly, "I don't know how to thank you enough, Mr. Ribar. My family and I will be forever indebted to you for this tremendous kindness. Thank you. Thank you very much."

"Markus, you are most welcome. I am so glad I could help you. I only hope that one day soon, our world will return once more to a sense of normalcy and decency."

The two men bid each other farewell, and Markus headed back home. A great weight had been lifted from him with the knowledge that he, his parents, and his siblings would be exempted from future deportations. What Markus did not know at the time was that, out of the approximately four thousand Jews in Bardejov, only 150 were granted this special work exemption. The others began being forcibly removed from their homes and deported to Poland just a few weeks later, in May 1942.

⁓⁓*⁓*⁓*⁓*⁓*⁓*⁓*

Rabbi Raphael Lowy, whose wife was an aunt of Anna Rosenberg, was the head representative of the Jewish community in Bardejov. Like other Jewish leaders throughout Slovakia, Rabbi Lowy frantically searched for ways to stop or at least delay the transports. After many long discussions, Lowy and several other Jewish notables in the town came up with a plan.

To force the issuance of a quarantine for Bardejov, a dozen or so Jews volunteered to be injected with a drug that created symptoms mimicking those of typhus. Even though it was a dangerous proposition for the volunteers, they bravely accepted the forced illness with the hope that it might stave off the impending deportations. Indeed, the district physician who examined the patients issued an official document verifying that there was a typhus outbreak in the town and declared that it was very dangerous to travel to or from Bardejov. The ploy was successful, and the transport was delayed—but only for a month.

Unfortunately, Hlinka officials learned that the outbreak was a hoax and identified Rabbi Lowy as the conspirator behind the ruse. Under the watchful eye of Stefan Reistetter, the chief Hlinka commander in Bardejov, the plans moved full speed ahead to transport the Jews of Bardejov out of Slovakia. Hundreds of horse-drawn carriages came from neighboring villages to take the Jewish families, which assembled in front of their homes, to the train station. The elite corps of Hlinka Garda, equipped with heavy arms, were also brought in from out of town to ensure that the Jews would not resist as they were loaded onto the trains, eighty-five souls per boxcar, without food or water. Reistetter made certain that Rabbi Lowy was one of the first Jews on the transport.

Bardejov town square May 15 or 16, 1942
Assembling Jews for deportation
Mrs. Israel Reich with her sons

Courtesy of the Bardejov Jewish Preservation Committee, Abraham Grussgott
Collection (published in Grussgott, Avrum.1998. *Bardejov Remembered: A Memorial
to the Jewish Community of Bardejov, Czechoslovakia 1734-1945*. Brooklyn, NY.)

Deportations continued until October 1942. By then, more than
fifty-eight thousand Slovak Jews had been sent away. However, reports
had begun filtering in that the Germans were murdering the Slovak Jews
in Poland in large numbers. A small delegation of Jewish citizens led by
Gisi Fleischmann and Rabbi Chaim Michael Dov Weissmandl assembled a
group of concerned individuals in the government and in the Vatican who,
through negotiations and bribery, were able to convince Tiso's government
to stop further transports. Slovakia became the first state under Nazi
influence to cease deportations. While the remaining twenty-four thousand

Slovak Jews breathed a very cautious sigh of relief, less than two years later, they would discover that the reprieve would only be temporary.

The years between 1942 and 1944 were precarious for the Jews who remained in Slovakia. While they had been spared from the dreaded transport, they were not free. The anti-Jewish measures and laws continued to be enforced. Jews could no longer own property or luxury goods and were forbidden from attending state schools. They had six p.m. curfews and weren't permitted to go to movies, parks, or the markets. Nor were they allowed to swim or attend sporting events. Because of the brutal and ruthless ways of the Hlinka Garda, merely the sight of the double cross—a symbol as important to the Hlinka as the swastika was to the Nazis—brought dread to the hearts of the Slovakian Jews. Even those who had the special economic exemption feared for their safety when walking in the streets. There were no privileges for the few Jews holding these certificates.

Rosenberg home (in the middle with a car in front)
in the town square of Bardejov, present day
Courtesy of Richard Rohan

The Rosenberg home on the town square was taken over by the government and given to a non-Jewish family. Forced to seek shelter elsewhere, Solomon, Anna, and their children ended up living in an acquaintance's converted garage.

Jews had to buy food on the black market, but because Erika was still young and didn't "look" Jewish, she would remove the Star of David from her coat and go to the market to purchase provisions for the family.

As a result of the prior deportations, very few Jewish boys were left in Bardejov. When they weren't working, Markus and his friend Bandi spent time together, especially on Shabbos. They'd walk on the side streets, always trying to stay out of the sight of the Hlinka Garda. Along the way, they'd talk about what was going on and how much they missed swimming in the Topka River and playing soccer in the park.

Prior to the war, Markus had been very involved in shul life, leading davening and, during the high holidays, singing in the choir at the main shul in town. He loved music, especially cantorial music. On those long walks, Markus would recall the famous *chazzans*, great talents who travelled to towns all over Eastern Europe to sing in synagogues. Their performances were entertainment for the Jewish townspeople, a sacred and uplifting form of entertainment, a distinctive blend of Jewish prayer and song. Markus, who considered himself a *ba'al tefilla*, relished the times he could be in the company of these highly talented and gifted men, hanging onto and savoring every note they intoned. But those days were long gone; that world no longer a reality for Markus.

While he and Bandi were hopeful that the transports had ceased indefinitely, they worried deeply about their own future and about those who had been forced away from their hometown. At the time, no one in Bardejov knew about Auschwitz or the other concentration camps that had sprouted up around Europe, camps designed to efficiently exterminate their friends and family and ultimately all the Jews on the continent. And no one from Bardejov knew yet that the vast majority of their family and friends who'd been deported in May of 1942 never made it to any particular destination. Instead, they'd been brutally murdered in the woods of Konska Wolya, near Opole in Poland.

During this period, Solomon wrote a letter to his brother-in-law Oscar in Texas.

"Beloved Oscar," the letter began, "Our world is on fire. We are persecuted every day. We have been forced out of our homes. So many of our friends and relatives have been forcibly sent off by train to unknown destinations. We hear of unspeakable things happening to them. We are so afraid. Only the Almighty knows what our future holds."

Deportation of Bardejov Jews
Gift of Abraham L. Grussgott, Museum of Jewish Heritage, NY

* ~ * ~ * ~ * ~ * ~ * ~ * ~ * ~ *

Three weeks later and six thousand miles away, Oscar Tanenbaum received the letter from Bardejov. As he read the pained words written by Solomon, his eyes filled with tears, and his head began throbbing. Leaning back, Oscar took a deep breath. Sitting quietly in his study for some time, he tried to sort out his thoughts. Oscar finally picked up the phone and called his attorney, Emil Cornbleth, one more time.

"Emil," Oscar began, "we just have to find some way to get my family out of Slovakia. I know that Sam Rayburn, the Speaker of the House, is very influential, probably even more than President Roosevelt. I'll bet he can help us, Emil. Don't you think he could?" Before Emil could respond, Oscar pressed on, "Would you please contact Mr. Rayburn and see if he can do something to get visas for my family? I am beside myself. I am so worried about their safety, I can't sleep even a minute at night. We've got to find a way to make this work."

"Of course, Oscar," Emil replied. "I'll send a letter to Mr. Rayburn right away and see what he can do."

Much correspondence went back and forth between Emil Cornbleth and Speaker Rayburn in the months that followed. Rayburn was sincere in wanting to help, but in the end, the visas did not materialize because of the severe restrictions placed on US visas as well as opposition in the US State Department to increasing the number of refugees allowed into the country. Ultimately, the Rosenbergs' fate was left in the hands of the countries waging a great war in Europe.

Chapter Six

In July 1944, the Russian army was closing in on the Nazis in eastern Slovakia. All Jews in the region, including those in Bardejov, were ordered to leave and move west, at least four hundred to five hundred kilometers from the area of combat.

The Rosenbergs, along with the remaining Jewish families in Bardejov, set out to find refuge elsewhere. Some families decided to hide in the woods in central and western Slovakia, hoping they would be safe there until the fighting was over. Some fled to Hungary, which was still untouched by the war. Others went to places in western Slovakia where they had family or friends.

The only person outside of Bardejov that the Rosenbergs knew well enough to contact was a candy salesman in the city of Zilina; he had been doing business with the family for years. This business acquaintance proved to be very helpful because he found a room that someone would rent out to them. All six members of the Rosenberg family shared this one small room, where they lived for several months.

Upon hearing the news about his family's relocation, Manny received permission from his army commander to take a short leave of absence to travel to Zilina. Manny feared greatly for their safety and was determined to help them escape from what he believed would be a horrible fate. He met and spoke with his father as soon as he arrived in the city.

"Please, Father," Manny implored, "you must leave this place now. It is not safe for you. It is not safe for mother or the children. I know something terrible will happen if you do not find a way out.

"We have options," he continued. "We can all go into the forest together. There are others out there already who will help us, partisans who are planning to fight against Tiso and his henchmen. We will be safe there until the fighting is done. I promise. People say the war is almost over. Please let us go now so we can survive. Please, Father, please. I beg that you do what is right."

Solomon looked thoughtfully at Manny and sat quietly for a few minutes, considering his son's proposal.

Then he looked over at Manny and said, "Son, I appreciate your great concern. I know you want to help. I know you think you have the right answer. But I just cannot take the family into the dangers of the forest. I do not think that is the solution. I believe in the Almighty, and I believe what will be will be."

"But, Father, you have no right to do this to the children," Manny cried. "Please think of them! At the very least, let me take Erika and Aaron. I will find somewhere for them to be safe."

Solomon looked at his wife. After a long silence, Anna softly answered, "You may take Erika with you but not Aaron. He is still too young. I absolutely will not allow my ten-year-old to wander around the forest. What will come to us will come to us."

Manny shook his head. With a great heaviness, he said, "All right then. Do as you will, my parents. I wish you well. Erika and I will need to go soon. I'll be waiting outside for her while she prepares to leave."

With that, Erika quickly packed

Erika Rosenberg

a small, worn travel bag with the few belongings she had brought from Bardejov. She then hugged her parents and little brother, Aaron, good-bye. Markus and David were out that afternoon, so she did not have the chance to bid them farewell.

As she walked downstairs to meet Manny, Erika's breath caught in her throat. She wondered when she would see her parents again. On the move with her brother, Erika had no idea what the future held.

Erika went with Manny to the place where he had been stationed, a town named Devinska Nova Ves. Manny had made several good acquaintances there, one of whom forged false papers for Erika, identifying her as a Christian. Once Erika was set up with the needed paperwork, Manny took her to the home of a family he had befriended, the Rocek family. An agreement had been made with the Roceks that Erika would pay a monthly fee to stay with them as well as spend her days working as their housekeeper. The arrangement wasn't ideal, but it was certainly preferable to deportation. Almost sixteen years old at the time, she accepted her lot with resolve and courage.

At one point during Erika's stay in Devinska Nova Ves, many parts of the town were bombed by the Germans. In the onslaught, the Roceks' home was hit, and the roof collapsed. Fortunately, everyone was in the cellar at the time. After escaping through a small window, the family and Erika moved into another house that was still under construction just outside of town. It was the only place they could live at that point, and while the situation was challenging, they did have shelter and food to eat.

During the time she was in the Roceks' charge, Erika tried to keep a low profile as much as possible. She could not, however, totally avoid interacting with those around her. When once asked by neighbors why she never went to mass, Erika blurted out, without any forethought, that she was Greek Orthodox and did not know anything about the Catholic church in Slovakia. Erika knew that she would have given herself away if she had gone to church, and the Rocek family would have been killed for harboring a Jew.

One day followed the next, and every night before Erika went to sleep, she offered prayers of gratitude for being sustained another twenty-four hours.

Toward the end of the war, when the Russians were driving the Nazis out of Slovakia, the city of Bratislava and its surrounding areas were bombed incessantly. Having nowhere safe to live during those days, Erika and some other people went to hide in a cave located just outside the town. Taking the small bit of food available to them, they hoped to stay there until the fighting was over. One night, a group of Russian soldiers happened upon the cave during a patrol. When they saw who was in there, the soldiers began forcibly removing all the young women, proceeding to take them to the woods near the mountains.

One soldier grabbed hold of Erika under her arm, pulling her up and roughly shoving her out of the cave.

"I'm so young," Erika implored to the Russian. "Why don't you let me go?"

The soldier pressed his body into Erika and growled in her ear, "Oh, I'm sure you have a boyfriend at home already."

For some unknown reason, the soldier let go of Erika at that moment. She began running as fast as she could, zigzagging off to the side rather than going straight ahead. The soldier reached for his gun and began shooting at her, but neither of them could see anything in the pitch black of night. Erika could hear the screams of the other young women being taken from the cave, but she ran farther and farther away.

Suddenly, Erika lost her footing and then no longer felt the earth beneath her. Desperately grasping for something, she managed to grab hold of a small bush, which immediately stopped her otherwise inevitable plummet off the side of a cliff down to the river far below. As she clung for her life, she held her breath and stayed completely silent. Though she heard the soldier still shooting, the gunfire was unquestionably slowing down. Finally, mumbling something angrily to himself, the soldier stopped firing and turned back to join his comrades.

Erika still didn't move. She wanted to be certain he was really gone. It seemed an eternity before the only sound she could hear was the water rushing along the riverbanks below her. Slowly and painfully, Erika dragged herself up from the cliff's edge.

Unable to see in the darkness, she finally found the entrance of the cave by crawling on the ground and feeling her way back. She entered and settled in a corner, trembling and exhausted. With her eyes wide open, she waited until the morning light brought a new day. Then, at last, she could rest.

None of the young women taken away that night by the Russian soldiers ever returned. Word got back that the women had been forced into the woods, raped, and then left for dead.

When the war was over in 1945, Erika had been separated from her family for nearly one year.

~~*~*~*~*~*~*~*

At the end of August 1944, a revolt broke out in western Slovakia. Partisans attempted to overthrow the pro-Nazi regime and re-establish the Republic of Czechoslovakia. As the partisan attacks intensified, the German army entered the country. Many Jews tried to reach the partisan-controlled areas, particularly around Banska Bystrica, hoping to help the rebels and hoping to survive.

Manny was determined to join the partisans. He deserted his post in the Slovakian army, but on his way to the mountains, he was stopped by some soldiers who demanded to see his papers. Manny began speaking in Slovak, trying to convince them that he was a gentile. But when they discovered he was circumcised, he was shipped off to Sered to a large Slovakian labor camp for Jews.

Markus also sought to join the partisans. He left his family in Zilina and successfully reached a group of rebels, staying in their camp for four weeks. During that time, the Russians were dropping food and ammunition from planes down into the mountains to help the partisans. But the partisan advances didn't hold, and when the Nazis came into the combat zone with their commandos and heavy armament, the entire uprising was crushed. Many partisans and Jews managed to flee farther into the mountains and remained there safely for the duration of the war. But many more, Markus included, were caught and sent off to the labor camp in Sered.

Meanwhile, David was taken off the streets in Zilina and thrown into the Jihlava prison near the capital city of Bratislava. A moat surrounded the prison, and machine guns fired throughout the night to ensure that no one would escape. From Jihlava, David was then transferred to Sered.

After the partisan revolt was suppressed, Tiso remained in office but in name only. Nazi Germany effectively took over Slovakia as an occupying force. With that change, the decision was made to resume Jewish deportations; this time, all Jews were to be sent out of Slovkia, regardless of their status, even if they held a certificate of exemption.

Solomon, Anna, and Aaron were still together, living in Zilina. They'd made it through Rosh Hashana and Yom Kippur, and in early October 1944, the holiday of Sukkos was fast approaching. To usher in the holiday, Solomon went to a nearby shul to daven. During services that night, Nazi soldiers surrounded the synagogue, rounded up everyone inside, and sent them straight to Auschwitz. When Solomon arrived at the camp the next day, he was instructed to go to the left. Within hours, Solomon's life was snuffed out in the gas chamber.

That same day, Nazi soldiers forcibly removed Anna and Aaron from their rented room in Zilina and sent them to Sered. They were temporarily reunited with David, but one week later, all three were sent in the same cattle car to Auschwitz.

The distance between the concentration camp and Sered was approximately one hundred kilometers, and the ride to the death camp did not take long. Once the train pulled into Auschwitz and the doors were opened, chaos ensued.

"Raus! Raus! (Out! Out!)," the *kapos* screamed at the frightened Jews.

German Shepherds barked and snapped at the newly arriving prisoners, and those who moved too slowly were hit over the head with wooden clubs.

As soon as they got off the train, Anna and Aaron were forced into the line for women, while David queued up with the men. Standing at the entry of the camp was a handsome, impeccably dressed Nazi officer with a boyish face and a calm demeanor. The man's name was Dr. Josef Mengele. When Anna and Aaron reached him, he politely pointed to the left. Please go to the left. Within hours, Anna and her ten-year-old son were dead, gassed by Zyklon-B, a cyanide-based pesticide.

Their transport was among the last to be gassed at Auschwitz. When the Nazis realized they were losing the war, they stopped operating the crematoria and tried to destroy the evidence of what, just weeks earlier, had been running at full capacity. At its peak of operation, the Nazi death machine at Auschwitz murdered some one thousand people per hour.

Aaron Rosenberg   Anna Rosenberg

When David made his way through the line to go into the camp, he was directed to the right. He entered through the gate and was almost immediately approached by Herman Garfein, a fellow Jew from Bardejov. Garfein was working in Auschwitz as a *schreiber*, counting those coming into the camp and recording names to be used at roll call. As often as he could, he would go to the selection point to warn people he knew of impending danger.

Garfein looked at David and told him that he was too skinny and too small to survive in Auschwitz. He went on to inform him that some laborers were needed in a factory near Breslau, about a six-hour train ride away from Auschwitz. At the factory, the workers were making wooden grenade cases for the German army. Garfein strongly advised David to take this opportunity to leave the death camp.

Though David had never done a single day of woodwork or carpentry in his life, he took Garfein's advice and volunteered for the job. By two p.m. the next day, David was on his way out of Auschwitz. He wasn't in the concentration camp long enough to receive a tattooed number.

David finished out the war working in this factory, completely unaware of what was happening in the concentration camp or to his family. When the Russians liberated Breslau, David came across a group of big trucks headed to Slovakia. After hitching a ride, he was back home in two days.

~~*~*~*~*~*~*~*

Manny entered Auschwitz on November 10, 1944. His trip to the camp had taken seven days, a good deal longer than it should have, because much of the train track between Slovkia and Auschwitz had been bombed out, and multiple detours had been required along the way. A great number of people on the transport died en route.

When he got off the train, Manny was sent to the right, branded with his new identity number, and assigned to a barrack. From the very first day, Manny was forced to do hard labor, backbreaking work in and around the camp. Over the months that followed, he was harshly beaten several times as well—both by kapos and by fellow prisoners, specifically Russian prisoners of war.

Manny quickly learned what was taking place in the camp. While rumors had been circulated about atrocities, no one on the outside could really comprehend the enormity of the destruction. No one could imagine that a nation as refined as Germany could create gas chambers and crematoria to facilitate murder of this magnitude. And until the cold facts were foisted onto the world, those on the outside could never really envision the evil the Nazis and their accessories inflicted upon millions of innocents.

Manny remained in Auschwitz until mid-January 1945. At that time, along with many others, he was sent on a three-day march. A large number of people died along the way. Those who survived were put on open cattle cars and sent to Germany. On the journey from Poland to Germany, many more died, and each time someone succumbed, he was thrown off the train into the snow to give the survivors a little more elbow room. Manny refused to let himself fall asleep on the long journey. Somehow he knew that, if he nodded off, he would freeze to death. Severely undernourished and wearing barely any clothes, Manny survived the train ride by setting his head on his elbow and watching the scenery pass by outside.

Shipped from one work camp in Plattling, Germany, to another in Mauthausen, Austria, Manny performed whatever manual labor he was ordered to do. On April 29, Manny was liberated by General Patton's Third Army. He suffered from typhus, as well as severe stomach problems and arthritis. He was very ill, and the doctors in the displaced persons camp sternly ordered him to throw away all candies, chocolate, cookies, and fruit given to him by sympathetic Allied troops; otherwise, he would surely die. Manny followed their orders and was brought back from the brink of death by first being sustained with the cooking water from rice and then eventually moving to soup and hot wheat cereal. Four months later, in August 1945, he was released from the hospital and sent by bus back to Slovakia.

⁓⁓*⁓*⁓*⁓*⁓*⁓*⁓*

Markus was sent to Auschwitz in mid-September 1944, before his parents and other brothers arrived. When transferred from Sered, Markus travelled in the same transport as two of his cousins, Benjamin Lowy and Jack Nagel. Their train arrived at the camp at around six p.m. When Markus reached the selection point, he was routed to the right.

However, his cousin Jack was accompanied by his young brother, and when the two reached the selection point, Josef Mengele looked at Jack and asked in German, "Is this your son?"

"No, he's my brother," Jack said.

"You go to the right," Mengele said courteously. "Your little brother will go to the left."

Jack hesitated. How could he separate from his brother without knowing the boy would be all right? Jack had always been there for his little brother, protecting him, making sure he felt safe. In that instant of indecisiveness, an SS guard forcibly pulled Jack's brother away and pushed him into the line of women, children, and elderly moving to the left. The little boy started screaming and crying. Jack didn't know what to do. He wanted to run to his brother's side and comfort him, but Jack was being shoved in the opposite direction. A few moments later, his brother was no longer in sight. Jack wondered where his brother would go once inside the camp and when he might see him again.

As Jack walked into Auschwitz with the others, he noticed on the horizon some smokestacks belching fire, smoke, and ash. *Perhaps it's some kind of factory*, Jack thought, *a steel factory*. An acrid odor permeated the air.

"What is it?" Jack asked a fellow walking next to him.

"Don't you know? It's people. They're burning people. All the old people—the children too. Anyone who can't work."

At that moment, Jack knew he had lost his brother forever.

Eventually, Jack caught up with Markus. Benjamin was right behind him. The three cousins were directed to a series of lines of men waiting to be processed and to receive their tattooed identity numbers. Jack and Benjamin were in one line; Markus was sent to another.

After a short time, Herman Garfein appeared and whispered something to Jack and Benjamin. As soon as Garfein left, the two young men began running. They dashed away so fast that they didn't even have time to tell Markus what they were doing. A moment later, Markus looked over his shoulder at the place where his two cousins had been standing. Seeing that they weren't there anymore, he turned his head further, looking around until he could make out the two turning a corner just up the way. Markus didn't know why they had left so suddenly, but he figured that, if his cousins were running away, he should probably do the same.

Markus caught up with Benjamin and Jack, and together the three of them came to a large barrack. All the barracks were built on stilts, so the three young men—cold, tired, and extremely hungry—crawled underneath to wait out the night. Once beneath the structure, they tried repeatedly, yet unsuccessfully, to find comfortable positions in which they could rest.

Markus asked Benjamin, "Why did you run?"

"You remember Garfein from Bardejov? He works here in the camp, and he told me to get out of there as fast as I could because the men in that line would be joining the Sonderkommando. I didn't know what he was talking about, so he told me those are the people who dispose of the bodies of dead Jews from the gas chambers and crematoria. He said the Nazis end up killing all the people in the Sonderkommando after a few weeks so there will be no eyewitnesses later on."

The three cousins fell silent, each burying himself in deep thought, trying to fathom the fate that had befallen them. There was nothing more to say that night.

After the long sleepless hours, morning arrived. Markus and his cousins were famished. Aching and bruised, they cautiously pulled themselves out from under the barrack and found a group of men who appeared to be on their way somewhere, hopefully somewhere to eat. The three cousins managed to blend in and soon found themselves in a line for breakfast. The meal consisted of a paltry piece of stale bread along with a small cup of a brown, tasteless liquid resembling coffee. Markus and his cousins would soon find out that those lucky enough to escape the gas chambers would be given just barely enough food to keep them alive. After breakfast the first morning in Auschwitz, a selection for work was conducted. Markus volunteered and spent the remainder of his time in and around Auschwitz doing hard labor.

Both Markus and Jack had smuggled money into the camp by wrapping it in thin rubber and hiding it in their rectums. During their stay in Auschwitz, the money was used to bribe kapos for some extra food. One time, when Jack had just procured a small loaf of bread, Markus asked if he could have some. Jack agreed but half-jokingly insisted that Markus pay back half of what it cost to buy the bread. Markus said he wouldn't repay the money, but he did promise to give half a loaf of bread back to Jack when they got out of the camp.

Most of Markus's days were spent dismantling wooden barracks and then lowering them into trucks and rail cars. This was all part of the Nazis' efforts to eliminate physical evidence of the atrocities they had committed.

In the end, the Nazis would not be able to conceal the evil they had done, no matter how hard they tried. And though Markus never received a tattooed number on his arm, the adversity and pain he experienced in Auschwitz would never be completely erased from his heart.

~~*~*~*~*~*~*~*

In late December 1944, the Russian army was only one hundred kilometers away and closing in on Auschwitz. Earlier Allied offensive drives had already prompted SS chief Heinrich Himmler to order all concentration camp prisoners evacuated toward the interior of the Reich. Germany did not want any prisoners falling into Allied hands and revealing the crimes of the Nazis. At the same time, some prisoners were still needed to keep the German war machine running as long as possible. For those too weak or too ill to even begin the evacuation marches, the Nazis either shot them dead, suffocated them in the gas chambers, or killed them by lethal injection.

In early January 1945, the prisoners from Auschwitz were taken into Germany. Along with five thousand to six thousand people, Markus marched out of the concentration camp into the brutal Polish winter. In the elements, without shelter, proper clothing, or food, Markus's group walked some one hundred to two hundred kilometers. The SS guards had strict orders to kill any prisoner who could not keep up. Thousands of prisoners died of exposure, starvation, and exhaustion along the way. In Markus's group, fewer than one thousand survived to reach their destination, a railway station. Those who endured the death march were put onto cattle cars and sent deep into Germany. They arrived at their destination, a city named Braunschweig, in mid-January 1945.

While they were there, Markus and his fellow survivors worked in a factory that serviced diesel and lift trucks. Soon after their arrival, the prisoners had to hide in ditches around ten each morning, because the American planes bombed the city. At night, the British planes dropped bombs as well. In between these attacks, the men spent time in blasted factories, salvaging nuts, bolts, and other pieces of equipment from the rubble, trying to clean the parts and box them up for use again. Markus remained in Braunschweig until April, when the Americans advanced into the area.

The prisoners were moved again, this time to a small camp near Winnenberg in northern Germany. On April 28, when the British army arrived at the camp, the German soldiers were suddenly nowhere to be found. Though Markus and his fellow prisoners did not immediately know who the British soldiers were, they quickly understood that the war was finally over.

Within a week or so of being liberated, about half of the former prisoners fanned out into the small town nearby, many of them going to peasants' homes, asking for whatever food they could spare. Because their starved bodies were not ready for the rich foods given to them by the townspeople, a large number of the former prisoners died in the streets. When the British soldiers saw this happening, they picked up the rest of the refugees, put them on trucks, and took them to a military camp in Winnenberg. For the next several months—May through July—some twenty thousand to thirty thousand former concentration camp inmates and prisoners of war were nursed back to health and brought back into the land of the living. At the time of liberation, Markus weighed less than ninety pounds.

Most European countries set up offices in trailers in the displaced persons camp, each with its respective flag waving on top. Dozens of nationalities were represented, with every country trying to identify its citizens in the camp. Since no one had official identification papers, no formal method was in place to determine where a displaced person had come from. Knowledge of a particular language was not necessarily proof of identity, because most Europeans were multilingual. The officials tried to verify nationality by asking where the refugees lived and presenting questions about the country's history and then determining whether the answers seemed factually accurate.

Markus went to the Czechoslovakian office and filed registration papers to go back to his home country. But he needed to be cleared medically before he would be allowed to leave the camp. Several months later when Markus's health improved in September 1945, he boarded a bus that took him from Germany to Prague.

Chapter Seven

On the night of January 19, 1945, Bardejov was liberated by a Russian army division led by a tall, handsome officer who was a Russian Jew named Captain Zaretsky. Seven local Jews who had managed to stay hidden in cellars beneath the town for the duration of the war crept out of their hiding places that night. Markus's best friend, Avrum Grussgott, was one of the seven. In the ensuing weeks and months, a slow trickle of surviving Jews returned to their hometown.

Anyone who had been part of the Hlinka party was taken prisoner by the Russians. When they came for Adam Ribar, the surviving Jews immediately spoke up on his behalf, acknowledging that, while he'd been a Hlinka party member, he'd also been a true friend to the Jews, helping them on many occasions. Consequently, Ribar was released by the Russians and allowed to return to his home.

By 1949, some three hundred to four hundred Jews were living in Bardejov, although not all of them were former inhabitants. The little town of Bardejov became a rehabilitation center for Jewish refugees and a transit point for immigration into Palestine.

~~*~*~*~*~*~*~*

After her departure from the Rocek family, Erika travelled to Bratislava. She found a city in chaos—people frantically searching for food and shelter and trying to locate family members who were missing. It was in this bedlam that Erika somehow managed to come across some old neighbors from Bardejov who offered her a place to sleep on their floor. The gesture was very kind, but Erika didn't feel right taking food and shelter from them when they did not have enough even for themselves.

Next door to these neighbors, however, was a soup kitchen, the place where all the refugees returning from the war had their first meals. Erika went into the building and asked if the kitchen needed any help. She was told she'd be provided with room and board if she would work there. Erika quickly agreed and got started right away. She spent her days waiting on people and cleaning tables, which gave her the opportunity to see everyone who passed through.

That is exactly how Erika happened upon her first sibling coming home. At first, they just stared at each other, unable to completely grasp that they'd both somehow survived. But then Erika and David embraced one another, relieved that they weren't alone in the world. Each asked about their parents and other siblings. Neither knew the fate of Markus or Manny at the time, but David was quite certain that their parents and little brother would not be returning. Remembering her rushed good-byes to her mother and father and Aaron over a year ago, Erika was greatly saddened by this news. Still, she and David knew they had no choice but to move forward.

David decided to stay with Erika in her small room until they could figure out where to go and what to do next. Planes were not flying, and almost no trains were running. No one had money, and there was no reliable way to get anywhere. Europe was still reeling from the aftereffects of the war.

After some time, Erika and David decided to try to return to Bardejov. With much effort, David managed to find a horse and buggy to take them there, but when they set out for their trip, the buggy got stuck every few blocks. After this happened many times over, they gave up and turned back to Bratislava. They needed another plan.

Because many of the Russian soldiers were peasants, they had never seen watches before and were fascinated with the small timepieces. David found a soldier who would let him get train tickets in exchange for a watch. When they arrived in Bardejov, the two siblings went to their aunts' home/grocery store, where Erika had grown up. Knowing now that their aunts must have been murdered in Auschwitz, Erika and David wanted to see who was occupying the house. After knocking on the front door, they waited in anticipation until a non-Jewish Slovak man answered. He and his family had moved into the home during the war. David and Erika explained their situation to him and asked if they could have a room in which to live. The man was sympathetic and agreed to the arrangement.

Once David was settled in Bardejov, he was eager to start working again. Without any resources to speak of, David needed creativity and a lot of luck. The first business venture he embarked on was the production and sale of cigarettes. David manufactured cigarettes from the dried tobacco plants harvested from wild fields. After that project, he decided to move back into the grocery business, focusing mainly on spices, pepper, baking powder, and vanilla. Determined to rebuild what had been lost during the war, David was up before dawn every morning. He would awaken Erika then as well to make sure both could get as much done as possible. Initially, David and Erika worked out of the home where they were staying.

One day in September 1945, Erika heard a knock at the door. She opened it up, and standing on the porch was her brother, Markus. Their eyes filled with tears. The sense of relief was palpable, knowing that they had each survived the nightmares of the war. Several months after Markus returned, Manny, too, came back to Bardejov. Still suffering from the effects of the illnesses and poor health conditions he had endured, Manny could barely walk. He spent many more months convalescing before he experienced a complete return to health. At some point after that, Manny decided to change his last name to *Rohan*.

All the surviving Rosenberg children lived in their aunts' former home, along with a few other relatives who had returned and the non-Jewish Slovak family. Though it was oftentimes a tumultuous living arrangement, everyone was very supportive of the others.

‿‿*‿*‿*‿*‿*‿*‿*

When the war was over, Oscar and Bernie Tanenbaum tried desperately to determine the fate of their family from Bardejov. Oscar was close with Jacob Lowy, who was a son of Rabbi Raphael Lowy, the former leader of the Jewish community in Bardejov. Fortunately, Jacob had ended up in London during the war, after he escaped Slovakia on a trainload of aluminum that he had been trying to sell. Had that not happened, Jacob likely would have ended up murdered by the Nazis alongside his father. Oscar enlisted Jacob's help to locate the whereabouts of any surviving Rosenbergs. But Europe was still in shambles, and Lowy was unsuccessful in his endeavors.

In the meantime, Markus came to understand the irrefutable ramifications of what the Nazis had done and wrote a letter to his cousin, Jacob, informing him of the family situation.

Dear Jacob,

You will certainly be surprised to receive my letter. I heard from your brother Benjamin that you are in communication with my uncle Oscar Tanenbaum in Texas and that he has sent to you a cheque for my sister, Erika. I am also told that you are making enquiries about my parents and the other members of our family. I would like to inform you about the tragedy which has met all of us during the oppression of the fascist regime.

First of all, I want to tell you that only the eldest brother Emanuel, myself, David, and our sister Erika have returned. From our dear father and our dear mother and also our youngest brother, Aaron, we had to take leave in the renowned Auschwitz, as they had to go to the left (which meant to the gas chambers), whereas we went to the right. At the moment we took leave of our parents, we knew that we shall never see them again. Our dear mother went hand in hand with your mother.

Our sister Erika remained in Slovakia, as she had forged documents as an Aryan, and in this way, she saved herself. We three brothers were actually saved by a miracle. We came to Auschwitz late in the war. We were therefore only seven months in the concentration camps and managed to overcome it.

We returned to Slovakia completely worn down so that my weight was only 40 kg, my brother Emanuel at 39 kg was lying ill with typhus, and my brother David weighed 42 kg. You can therefore imagine in what state we were. We came practically naked. All our belongings have disappeared, and we have not found anything from the flat and so on. I do not think that it is necessary to give further details about our position.

Concerning our relatives, I am sorry to say that out of the whole family Rosenberg, nobody returned except us. If you wish to write us, our address is Family Rosenberg, Bardejov, Presovska 5, Slovakia.

All the best wishes for a Happy New Year for you and your family, for our uncles and their families.

We remain,

Rosenbergs

Jacob forwarded a copy of Markus's letter to the Tanenbaums in America. As soon as the Tanenbaum brothers knew that their niece and three of their nephews had survived the war, they began sending money, food, and care packages—doing whatever they could to help out.

The returning Rosenberg men were the age of conscription into the army, but because their parents were no longer alive, the brothers were exempted from military service so they could financially support their family. Markus joined David in his start-up grocery business, a new business that bore a new name, ARO—three letters taken from Markus's given name, *Abraham ROsenberg*.

The business grew, necessitating additional employees and a bigger facility. The Rosenbergs moved the operation out of the house and opened up a real factory to keep up with the growth. With their business success, the Rosenbergs began making money, a good deal of money, some of which they reinvested in the company (buying new equipment and product), and some of which they sent to their uncle in the United States for safekeeping. Though life was moving forward in a positive way for them in Bardejov, they felt the need for a safety net in America should the situation change in Europe once more.

While it was devastating to come back to Bardejov and find so few survivors from the town, Markus and others were determined not to provide Hitler with a posthumous victory. Markus was also determined not to give up on Jewish life, Jewish tradition, and Jewish belief, despite what had happened in Europe and how this tragedy had reshaped his own personal religious outlook.

In the years after the war, Markus and his close friend Bandi helped others bring Jewish life back to Bardejov. Makeshift religious schools were set up in town. Jews began davening in shul again. People who wanted to immigrate to Palestine were helped financially; some even received military training before departing so they could serve in the fledgling Jewish state's fight for independence.

On May 14, 1948, when the new state of Israel was announced, the Jews of Bardejov came together and made an Israeli flag, which they proudly hoisted on top of a post at the home of Markus's good friend, Avrum Grussgott, who lived on the town's main street. A tangible excitement filled the air, with many of the Jews in town passionately talking about and making plans to move to the new Jewish country.

* ~ * ~ * ~ * ~ * ~ * ~ * ~ * ~ *

Around 1947, the political landscape began to change radically in Czechoslovakia. Because the country had been liberated by Russia and because there were residual bad feelings about how the West had treated Czechoslovakia before the war, the country was squarely under the sphere of Soviet influence. The Communist parties in Czechoslovakia were making tremendous inroads in their quest to take over the government. And while this was all taking place, Markus began thinking that perhaps the United States might be the better place to live in the long run.

In the winter of 1948, Markus and Erika were in Switzerland sending more money to their uncle in America and making arrangements to have a lift—a large container of furniture, china, silver, crystal, carpets, and jewelry—transported out of Czechoslovakia. The Rosenbergs wanted these items to be safe in case the Communists took over the country, On

February 28, while Markus and Erika were still in Switzerland, they heard the dreaded news over the radio: the Communists had taken power over the Czechoslovakian government. Markus immediately called David in Bardejov. Their conversation was brief. David simply said, "Stay where you are, and don't come back."

Markus and Erika never returned to Bardejov. With only one suit and two shirts in his possession, Markus's life in Czechoslovakia abruptly ended.

Shortly thereafter, Markus and Erika travelled from Switzerland to Brussels, Belgium, transferring their papers to the American consulate to begin the steps needed to immigrate to the United States. Understanding that this process might take a good deal of time, Markus rented an apartment for himself and his sister until their visas to America would be received.

David Rosenberg circa 1948

David and Manny were still in Czechoslovakia, waiting to see what material changes would come about with the Communists in control. It did not take long to realize that Czechoslovakia was once again spiraling downward, this time under a new set of totalitarian rulers. Dissidents from all levels of society were purged. The ideological principles of socialism and communism began to pervade intellectual and cultural life. And the Communists, committed to an economy that was centrally controlled, set out to abolish all private ownership of capital.

A number of months after the Communist takeover of Czechoslovakia, David awoke very early in the morning and hired the only cab in Bardejov to take him to the train station. Once he arrived in Bratislava and attained some false identity papers, he departed for France. David left everything—the entire business and all the family possessions. He stayed in France with a close relative, Jack Reich, for several years until his request to enter the United States was processed and approved in 1953.

~~*~*~*~*~*~*

When David left Bardejov, Manny was in Prague. Not long after David departed, the Communists arrested Manny and threw him into jail. As the sole brother left to represent the family grocery business, he was a capitalist. Not only that but Manny was also trying to send a lift out of the country with the family's valuables. Such actions were not to be tolerated in the new communist regime. Manny remained incarcerated for several months while Markus tried to figure out a plan to secure his release.

Markus could not go back to Czechoslovakia, because he too would have been put in jail. After all, he was also a business owner, a capitalist. Someone else needed to help Manny. Consulting with his cousin Jacob in London, Markus determined that it would be best to send Erika, because she was female and therefore likely to raise little suspicion.

When Erika reached Prague, she found the city in a state of anarchy. There was no rule of law, no one to talk to, and no official channel to go through. She would have to figure everything out by herself.

Erika contacted a lawyer she had heard could help Manny. This lawyer knew the jailer with the keys to Manny's cell, but it became obvious that a very large sum of money would be needed to convince the jailer to set Manny free. Because Erika did not have much cash with her in Czechoslovakia, Markus had to finagle some financial assets, moving money from one country to another so that the transactions would remain under the radar. When the funds finally made it to Erika, Markus warned her not to give the money directly to the jailer. He worried that the prison official would pocket the bribe and still not let Manny go.

Erika had a decision to make. If she gave the money to the jailer and Manny was not released, Markus would be incredibly angry with her. But if she didn't give the money to the jailer, then Manny would never get out. She was there to help her brother, and doing so was going to involve some degree of risk. In the end, Erika decided to give the money to the lawyer, who, after taking his share, gave the rest to the jailer. The jailer in turn released Manny.

Manny met Erika outside the prison. She had been instructed by the lawyer to hand him a train ticket and then walk away. She was not to talk to him or acknowledge him in any way. But Manny didn't follow the plan. He protested and said he wanted to get the merchandise from the lift to send to America. Fuming at her brother's nonchalant attitude, Erika ordered him to get out of the city as fast as he could and avoid showing his face to anyone. After all, she had risked her life in

Erika Rosenberg and Manny Rohan in Prague

coming back to Czechoslovakia to rescue him, and she wasn't about to go through that again. So that's what Manny did; Erika gave him no choice. They left, and the family valuables never made it out of the country.

⁓⁓*⁓*⁓*⁓*⁓*⁓*⁓*

At no time had Manny ever intended to move to the United States. Prior to the Communist takeover, he was geared for diplomatic service and had planned on staying in Czechoslovakia. President of the student body at the University of Prague, Manny went to all the garden parties and balls for the American Embassy. But those plans changed when Manny became a wanted man. One of his close friends, Michael Petrak, worked at the American Embassy in Czechoslovakia and was instrumental in having Manny's papers processed so he could leave the country expeditiously. Manny departed Czechoslovakia within days of his release from prison, and while he was the last Rosenberg to leave the place of his birth, he was the first of the Rosenberg siblings to arrive in America.

Erika returned to Brussels to wait with Markus until they received permission to emigrate. Markus was unsure of when, or even if, they would be allowed to go to America, so he filed paperwork to go to other countries, such as Bolivia, to ensure that, at some point, they would at least be able to leave Europe. Finally, the day arrived when they were permitted to set out for America, with Oscar and Bernie Tanenbaum guaranteeing their sponsorships. Markus and Erika were thrilled.

The two travelled by boat on the *Queen Elizabeth*, departing from Cherbourg, France. Three classes of travel were available on the boat— third class (with ten to twelve people sharing a room), second class (with four people to a room), and first class. Markus did not want to spend too much on the journey, so he purchased a third class ticket for himself. But he also didn't want Erika to travel in less-than-ideal conditions, so he purchased a second-class ticket for her. On May 11, 1949, Markus and Erika reached the new country, disembarking in New York.

Part Two

The New Country

Chapter One

Oscar Tanenbaum's daughter, Frances, was living in Spring Valley, New York, when Markus and Erika arrived. She hadn't seen her cousins in more than ten years, since she was a child visiting Europe.

Markus had needed some dental work for a while and was having a great deal of discomfort. Because Frances's father-in-law was a dentist who spoke Yiddish, Markus decided to have the dental work done in New York rather than wait until he arrived at his intended destination: Dallas, Texas, where Oscar Tanenbaum and his wife, Rose, had moved around 1947. Markus and Erika stayed with Frances's in-laws until Markus was feeling better and ready to make the last leg of their journey.

When Markus and Erika arrived in Dallas, they reunited with their aunt and uncle at their home on Beverly Drive in Highland Park, an upscale Dallas suburb. Seeing Oscar and Rose in person was a tearful, joyous moment for Markus and Erika. Everyone felt a great sense of relief, and the two new immigrants stayed in the grand home on Beverly Drive until Markus found an apartment on South Boulevard some weeks later.

Neither Markus nor Erika spoke more than a few words of English, and while they strove to learn the language of their new country, they also sought out those who could speak to them in their mother tongues— Czech, Yiddish, Slovak—so they wouldn't feel quite so different from everyone else around them. During those early days, the love and attention

Oscar and Rose gave to their niece and nephew helped smooth over the inevitable bumps they faced while acclimating to a new culture.

Not long after Markus moved into the new apartment, he met a new friend, Sol Prengler. Sol had emigrated from Ludow, Poland, a town very close to Treblinka. Though Sol was nearly twenty years older than Markus, the two men formed a deep friendship almost immediately. Because they lived across the street from one another on South Boulevard, Markus and Erika would go to Sol's house almost every evening, sit outside on the large porch, drink lemonade, and discuss life. They talked about business. They exchanged views on Jewish causes. Together they spoke about what had happened in Europe and shared their personal experiences and losses during the war. With their similar backgrounds and attitudes toward Judaism, Markus and Sol became as close as brothers. Markus also spent time every day with Oscar, his dear uncle who, along with Uncle Bernie, had worked so long and so hard to make sure their nephews and niece would arrive safely in the United States.

Within several months of settling in Texas, Markus was ready to start working and anxious to get involved again with wholesale groceries. He began looking for business opportunities and discovered that the Quartermaster Corps, the organization responsible for providing noncombat supplies to the US army, was accepting bids for a new black pepper contract. Because Markus still did not speak English fluently at that time, Oscar helped him gather the information needed to submit the bid. Using some of the money he and his brothers had transferred to the United States from Europe, Markus secured the letter of credit required for the bid.

"What should I write down for your company name, Markus?" Oscar asked.

"Well, in Bardejov," Markus said, "we called ourselves ARO after the war. A-R-O for my name, Abraham Rosenberg."

"Interesting. Well, there's a word in English—arrow—that sounds just like your old company name. But this word is like a bow and arrow. What do you think of using that word?"

Markus thought for a moment.

"A bow and arrow? Arrow ... Yes, that's good. Very good. Let's do that," Markus said as he nodded in approval.

Markus did not know that his bid would be competing with those from national companies such as McCormick, French's, and Durkee. At the time, he did not know much at all about these other companies. He only knew that, if he won the bid, he'd be able to start his own business.

Markus went to New York City to attend the Quartermaster bidding process. At ten a.m., the sealed bidding letters began being opened. Tension filled the room as Markus stood there with representatives from all over the country. One by one, the letters were cut open and the bids tabulated. When the last bid was recorded, the Quartermaster officer stood up to speak.

"The lowest bid received today is from Arrow. Is there a representative from the Arrow company here with us now?"

Markus raised his hand.

"I am from Arrow," he proclaimed in his thick Czechoslovakian accent.

"What is your business address in Dallas, sir?"

"I don't have one yet, sir," Markus answered. Snickers of laughter could be heard around the room. Markus plowed ahead. "I have the bond, sir. If I get the bid award, I will wire to you when I get back to Dallas, where I will make the pepper."

With a skeptical look, the officer informed Markus that, before he could begin processing the pepper, his facility would need to be inspected and approved for proper sanitation.

"It is fine, officer, sir. I will have the building for you in one week, and then you will come look at it," Markus promised.

"Okay, you are the lowest bidder, so we will give you seven days to answer us," the officer said before leaving the room.

Markus turned around and, without looking at anyone, immediately went down to Lafayette Street in Manhattan where he purchased a pepper grinder and the canning filling needed to process the order. After arranging to have the equipment shipped to Dallas, Markus called Oscar.

"I got the bid! I got the bid! But now I need a place to work, and I need it right away," Markus told him excitedly.

A few days later, with his uncle's help, Markus secured a new place of business: 2815 Main Street in downtown Dallas. Right away, Markus wired the Quartermaster Corps to inform it of his new location. Two days after that, when Markus went to open up the building, the inspector from the Quartermaster stood outside and looked at Markus with a confused expression.

"Is this Arrow?"

The building did not yet bear a company sign, and when the visitor peered through the window, he saw that the inside was completely empty.

"Yes, it is Arrow, but please let me explain the situation to you," Markus said.

Markus told the inspector his story, and the inspector gave him approval to start working on the pepper contract. Markus went down to the Texas Employment Agency that afternoon and hired two young women—sisters in fact, Eloisa and Frances Carrasco—to help him start the pepper processing. Erika also joined the effort, and the four of them together ground the pepper, processed it, and then packaged it in the cans. The first employees of Arrow filled the pepper order on time for the US army and, along the way, sneezed more than they ever had in their lives.

Chapter Two

❦

The early 1950s were positive, transformative years for the Rosenberg siblings. From the old country, they brought with them a contagious work ethic as well as an unbounded resilience and drive for success. In the new country, they no longer felt burdened or restrained as they had during World War II and the Communist takeover. The Rosenbergs were now free to pursue their dreams in business, start their own families, and fully embrace a life without limits imposed by others.

Erika didn't learn English as quickly as Markus did, and she had a more difficult time adjusting socially to living in Texas. She felt she'd be better off in New York, at least until she was better acclimated to American culture. In New York, she was introduced to a Hungarian Holocaust survivor, Andy Sigel. After a number of months, Erika and Andy decided to marry. In 1953, they wed in Uncle Oscar and Aunt Rose's home in Dallas. The wedding was beautiful, especially because the family was there together.

Erika and Andy Sigel's wedding

From left to right: David Rosenberg, Markus Rosenberg, Bernie Tanenbaum, Andy Sigel, Oscar Tanenbaum, Morris Goldfinger, Manny Rohan

Erika and Andy Sigel's wedding

Back row from left to right: Markus Rosenberg, Rose Tanenbaum, Oscar Tanenbaum, Erika Rosenberg Sigel, Andy Sigel, Etsy Kogut, Manny Rohan, Rose Tanenbaum, Bernie Tanenbaum, David Rosenberg
Front row: Sarah Lenowitz

Erika and Andy Sigel's wedding
From left to right: David Rosenberg, Andy Sigel, Manny Rohan, Markus Rosenberg

David had recently arrived from France, where he'd been living for several years after fleeing from Communist Czechoslovakia. In late 1956, he would meet Gusta (Gussie) Steiman in Toronto. They would marry in January 1959 and then settle in Dallas. Three sons would be born to them: Sheldon (Shelly), Bernard (Bernie), and Oscar.

Manny was also in Dallas for Erika and Andy's wedding. When he had first arrived in America, he had moved to Austin, Texas, where Uncle Bernie Tanenbaum and his family lived. After taking Manny into their home, Bernie's wife, Rose, had treated him like a son. Manny was lost and still vexed by his experiences in the war; Aunt Rose helped him reclaim his life. In time, Manny was back doing what he loved most: learning. Enrolled at the University of Texas at Austin, Manny began taking courses that would prepare him for law school. In time, Manny married Valerie Rosenwaser, sister of Markus's childhood friend, Bandi. After living in Canada for several years, they also came to settle in Dallas in 1959 and had two children, Audrey and Richard.

Markus, Manny, and David

Chapter Three

❦

The pepper contract led to another contract with the Quartermaster, this time for ketchup. Producing ketchup was a first-time venture for Markus and David, but that didn't impede them in any way. The project was completely in alignment with their philosophy of getting the business first and then figuring out how to deliver the goods. David and Markus were determined and confident that they would succeed. They formulated a recipe for the ketchup, and acquired new equipment to cook and bottle the product.

Bernie Tanenbaum's daughter, Etsy, and her husband, Reuben, were visiting Dallas from Austin when Markus and David were beginning their ketchup project. Reuben was in the insurance business and decided one day to call on his entrepreneurial cousins. He wasn't sure what he would find when he walked into Arrow, but he certainly wasn't expecting what he saw when he opened the front door.

There was David, standing on top of a stepladder next to a huge vat. Inside the vat was ketchup. Under different circumstances, Reuben might not have known the contents of the vat without first peering inside. But that day, he could easily tell what was cooking because David was covered from head to toe in ketchup. Apparently, they had encountered a minor glitch in the production of the tomato-based condiment, but certainly not enough of a glitch to prevent Arrow from producing the ketchup order and delivering it to the US army.

Not long after the delivery, David and Markus learned of another glitch in their production efforts. As the ketchup was being distributed to various army bases, the bottles' lids began popping off randomly—in the delivery boxes, on the tables in the mess halls; ketchup bottles were popping open everywhere. This was the occasion when David and Markus learned how useful it would have been had they vacuum-sealed the bottles before shipping.

⁓⁓*⁓*⁓*⁓*⁓*⁓*⁓*

After finishing college and military service in Korea, Victor Trubitt moved to Dallas from Chicago. Victor started working at a local accounting firm, and he and his wife were getting settled in their new home. One day while taking a walk, Victor ran into a business colleague.

"How's it going, Victor? Are you getting used to living in Dallas?"

"Yeah, it's good. Really good. The winters are certainly better down here. And things are going well at work too."

"That's great to hear, Victor. I'm happy for you. Say, Victor, I want to ask you about something. You see, I've got this account, and I just don't know what to do with it."

"What do you mean?"

"Well, it's these two brothers. They have this business where they sell spices—you know, pepper and things like that. Anyway, they're always hollering at each other. And they don't speak English over there. And I'm having a really hard time figuring out how to deal with them."

"Well, what is it they want to do accounting-wise?" Victor asked. "And how much are they willing to pay for the job?"

Victor's colleague explained the situation, and Victor decided he'd like to meet these two brothers and see if he could work out some arrangement with them. That's when Victor was introduced to David and Markus Rosenberg. Their visit was productive, and Victor became Arrow's new accountant.

In Markus and David, Victor found two brothers who were equally passionate about their business. And that passion often carried over to their conversations and decision making. Victor was American, so from his upbringing, it did seem like Markus and David hollered at each other a lot. However, the two brothers were eastern European, and emotional exchanges were part of their cultural upbringing. Both Markus and David were headstrong, and when they didn't agree on a particular decision or approach, the volume of their discussions heightened and could become quite animated. Nevertheless, what might appear to outsiders to be a volatile situation generally cooled quickly.

David and Markus were very close, very brotherly. Together, they were fashioned to be the perfect team to build an exceedingly successful business.

⁓⁓*⁓*⁓*⁓*⁓*⁓*⁓*

While in Bardejov during the years after the war, Markus and David had wired around $150,000 to their uncle Oscar in Texas for safekeeping. When the siblings left Europe and came to America, these funds were used to launch their business.

Arrow started with pepper, but the profits were nominal. More was needed to propel the business forward. Markus and David invested significant dollars to set up the type of robust spice line model they had in Czechoslovakia. Still, they had trouble breaking into the markets with the volume in sales needed. These growing pains, coupled with ventures like the exploding ketchup bottles, ate through their funds. Uncle Oscar and a distant relative, Sam Reichman, helped the brothers with additional funding, but Arrow still struggled until one day they got the notion of going into the dried bean business.

Dried beans—black beans, great northern beans, pinto beans, black-eyed peas—were the mainstay of Benham and Company, a twenty-year-old business based out of Mineola, Texas. In the world of beans, Benham was king at that time. Markus and David saw an opportunity and set their sights on capturing some of that business.

Abe Meyer, a Jewish grocery businessman in Dallas, was one of the first customers to buy large quantities of product from Arrow, initially for his own grocery stores, Cliff Food, and then for the much larger regional buying group, Affiliated Food Stores, which served independent grocery stores in several states. Influential in local politics as well as business, Abe served on the Dallas County Grand Jury, spent four years on the Dallas City Council, and was president of the Oak Cliff Chamber of Commerce, as well as the Lion's Club. While some of the other local Dallas Jewish businessmen were not helpful at all to Markus and David, Abe was different in this regard, taking an immediate liking to the two brothers and, as their friend, opening up many doors in the Dallas area and beyond.

Markus and David worked day and night to make the bean endeavor successful, each brother settling into the role that best suited his natural talents and abilities.

David was the sales force of Arrow. On the road most of the time, he sold product out of the back of his car in the early days. Too often, customers were insulting to him, mocking his European accent, berating him and calling him names, and sometimes even taunting his being Jewish. If these behaviors bothered David, no one ever would have known. He was a salesman par excellence. If a customer closed the door, David crawled through the window. He knew how to get a deal. And as long as he got a deal, the customer could say anything he wanted to David, insulting or not. David knew how to sell. Without the sales, Arrow would not be successful.

Likewise, if Markus could not figure out a way to effectively produce and deliver what David sold, Arrow would not be profitable. Markus ran the business from the inside, dealing with the purchase of raw material, production, and then delivery to the customer. He was adept at buying quality product at the best possible price. In addition, after thoroughly researching all different types of equipment, he would select the most effective packaging and processing machinery he could buy. Markus was also a master of efficiencies. Shaving a cent or two off the cost of producing a bag of beans might not have seemed like much, but over time, Markus knew that those pennies could make a significant difference in the bottom line.

Around 1954, Arrow got a very big break—an account with the Kimball grocery store chain. This deal solidly set the fledgling business on the path of solvency.

Chapter Four

❦

The 1950s marked the height of business for hotels and bungalows in the Catskill Mountains of upstate New York. Fondly called the "Borscht Belt," this area catered to Jewish New Yorkers, mostly *Ashkenazi* immigrants who enjoyed socializing and spending time away from the busy city life. Young adults would often go to the Borscht Belt to look for potential spouses.

Markus was in the Catskills in the summer of 1954, and it was there that he met a beautiful young woman named Ann Pappenheim. Originally from Vienna, Ann had immigrated to the United States as a young child. She came from a very prominent Jewish family of Austria-Hungarian lineage, a family committed to tra-

Markus Rosenberg

ditional religious observance. In Europe, the Pappenheim family was engaged in many Jewish causes, including the Vaad Hatzalah. Ann's father's involvement in this clandestine organization in the 1930s helped to ensure that boats filled with Russian, Polish, and other European Jews travelling illegally to Palestine would successfully reach their destination. Because of strict enforcement of quota limits by the British, the journeys of these passengers were fraught with danger.

Though he lived in Austria, Ann's father, Maurice Pappenheim, had French citizenship, because he had been born in France during the five-year window when his father worked in Paris as a wine merchant. In 1939, as the Nazis clamped down with even more extreme measures on Jews living under the Reich, a concerned Jew in the United States sent notification to Vienna that sponsorships were available for ten families active in Jewish communal welfare to come to America. Because of the political situation in Europe, an explosion of refugees, mostly Jewish, were trying desperately to get to America in the mid-to-late 1930s. However, for a variety of reasons, America had strict quotas on the number of German and Austrian immigrants allowed into the country. Being a French national enabled Ann's father and his family to leave Austria on one of those ten sponsorships. The other members of Ann's family who were unable to escape Europe at that time ultimately perished in the Holocaust.

When Ann met Markus in the Catskills, she was going out with one of Markus's friends. That relationship did not last, and when it was over, Markus called Ann to see if she would go on a date with him. Ann agreed. Markus had broken his arm playing volleyball while in the Catskills and ended up staying in New York longer than he had originally planned. During that period, Ann and Markus went out several times. When Markus returned to Dallas, their relationship developed, despite the long distance, over the course of many phone conversations and several trips that Markus took to New York to court Ann. For a year and a half, they dated, and on July 29, 1956, the two were married in New York City.

Wedding photos of Markus and Ann

That same year, Arrow incorporated for the first time, formally named Arrow Spice and Food. This was also the year that Arrow moved from their rented facilities (first on Main Street and then on Lamar Street) into a building the company purchased at 5051 Sharp Street. Along with that move, Markus and David acquired a nearby five thousand–square foot warehouse to accommodate their growing business.

Markus and Ann settled in Dallas. In May 1957, their first child was born, a girl named Helen. Nearly a year

Marcus and Ann Rosenberg with Maurice Pappenheim (Ann's father)

and a half later, a son named Steven came along. Three more daughters would follow in the 1960s—Margot, Elizabeth (Lizzy), and Sheri.

During this time, when Markus was fully engaged in planting roots and establishing his new life in the United States, he decided to change the spelling of his name to *Marcus*.

Part Three

❦

The Business

Chapter One

$\mathcal{I}$n the early 1960s, the bean business began to flourish at Arrow; the business growth was developed by David and his sales team. Recognizing the needs in the marketplace, David, along with Marcus, responded accordingly. Additional varieties of beans—cream peas, kidney beans, Michigan navy beans, speckled lima beans, and more—were added to the product line, as were popcorn and different types of rice. David was always on top of whom Arrow was selling to, who was paying, and who was not. He was a master at opening the door to new opportunities and sealing the deal. David travelled constantly and took very good care of the customers. When he visited any particular geographic area, Arrow could always count on a spike in sales from the customers in that locale.

Long gone were the days of David selling product out of his car trunk; Arrow began using various shipping companies to send orders to its customers. The more Arrow shipped, the more dissatisfied Marcus became with the delivery setup and the expense and inconsistency associated with it. To that end, Arrow decided that investing in its own trucks would make sense over the long-term. Arrow purchased a small fleet of trucks to deliver its orders and hired additional personnel, as well, to maintain the vehicles.

The list of customers grew from those in the surrounding areas to others spread across the country. Trucks would leave the warehouse full of product to deliver and then come back empty, ready to be filled again. This new arrangement created much more consistency in the delivery process.

But as time went on, Marcus saw new inefficiencies. The trucks were coming back empty. It would be better, he reasoned, if somehow the trucks returned filled up with product to be distributed to other parts of the country. If this could be achieved, the transportation costs for the company would be greatly reduced. Marcus's challenge became finding a way to utilize the backhauls. What could fill the trucks' trailers on the way back from their deliveries? The solution, he thought, might be in Paris, Arkansas, where a charcoal plant was up for sale.

Never having dealt with charcoal, Marcus travelled to Paris to meet the proprietor of the plant. He was taken around the factory to learn about the industry and how the plant was set up to crush lump charcoal and process it into briquettes. The owner offered to stay on and

Arrow delivery trucks

continue managing the operation if Arrow would purchase his plant.

Marcus thought about the potential opportunities of going into the charcoal business, which included the utilization of Arrow's delivery truck backhauls, and agreed to move forward. Papers were drawn up, and the deal was signed. The very next week, that charcoal plant in Paris burned down to the ground, and its former owner disappeared. Marcus was left with a piece of land in Arkansas and a piece of paper showing ownership of a plant that was still smoldering.

While this type of setback might have rattled others, it did not stop Marcus from going ahead with his plans. Another charcoal processing plant was built on the site; this one was more modern than its predecessor, and Marcus sought new management for the operation. He hoped the next overseer of the plant would be Andy Sigel, Erika's husband.

At the time, Erika and Andy were living in New York with their three children Gary, Kenny, and Karen. Andy was running a Laundromat and knew nothing about the charcoal business. Still, the opportunity to grow a new division at Arrow was quite appealing, and soon the Sigel family was moving to Arkansas.

Arrow's charcoal plant in Paris, Arkansas

Andy managed the operation, and business began growing, with customers coming from all over to purchase the charcoal. In the early 1960s, a young entrepreneur from Rogers, Arkansas contacted Andy and ordered three pellets of charcoal. When he tried to order more at a later time, he asked Andy if he could buy on credit. The order was small, and Andy did not have much confidence in the man's ability to pay back the money owed, particularly because he had tried to return charcoal left over from the previous season. Andy declined extending the credit.

Clearly disappointed with the decision, the man said, "One day, you'll be very sorry you didn't do business with me." And with that, Sam Walton walked out the door.

~~*~*~*~*~*~*~*

Jewish life was nonexistent in Paris, Arkansas, and in the beginning, spending religious holidays with the Rosenbergs in Dallas filled the void. But as the Sigel children grew older, their parents became more concerned about their lack of Jewish exposure. A military base, Fort Chaffee, was located near Paris, and on that base was a chaplain whom Andy befriended. Andy asked the chaplain if he would teach his children to read Hebrew. When the chaplain agreed, Andy went home to tell Kenny and Gary about the upcoming lessons.

"Dad, why are we going to learn Hebrew?"

"Because, Kenny, I learned Hebrew when I was a boy, and it would be good for you to learn too," said Andy.

"But, Dad," Kenny said, "how do you know if my children will even be Jewish?"

Andy did not have an answer for him. Not long after that, Andy's other son Gary asked, "Dad, how am I ever going to find a wife here if there aren't any Jewish girls?"

After six years in Arkansas, Erika and Andy began giving serious thought to how and where their children were being raised. They decided to give the day-to-day plant management over to Don Reeder, a local man who was quite skilled in this field. Then the Sigel family moved to Memphis, where the children were enrolled in a Jewish day school. From that point on, Andy managed the charcoal business remotely.

Over the years, Arrow purchased about a dozen charcoal plants, all but three located in Arkansas. One of those was in east Texas, another in Oklahoma, and the third in Roaring Spring, Missouri. Nearly all the plants were involved in manufacturing huge logs of carbonized charcoal, most of which was shipped to Paris to be processed into briquettes.

Andy, and eventually his son Gary, managed the entire charcoal division at Arrow, which constituted 10 to 15 percent of the company's overall business.

~~*~*~*~*~*~*~*

Manny worked at Arrow as well, along with Marcus in the production area. At the same time, Manny also pursued furthering his academic studies. In 1952, he earned a bachelor's degree from Southern Methodist University. In the late 1960s, he began law school at the age of forty-eight. He continued working at Arrow in the afternoons while going to classes in the morning and preparing his schoolwork in the evenings. In December 1972, he received his law degree and then set up his own practice.

Manny remained involved at Arrow, particularly with issues involving personnel, insurance, worker's compensation, threats to unionize, and other legal matters.

˜˜*˜*˜*˜*˜*˜*˜*

On June 12, 1963, Arrow planned to break ground on a new one hundred thousand–square foot facility in Carrollton, Texas, just outside of Dallas. The fourteen- or fifteen-acre site would include general offices, a manufacturing plant, and warehouse facilities. Railroad tracks would lead right up to the factory. Beans would be shipped in from all over the country directly to the Arrow's doors for processing, packaging, and distribution to grocery stores across the nation.

Marcus called David on the phone one evening before the groundbreaking and exclaimed, "David, I have some good news for you."

"What is it, Marcus?"

"Governor Connally is going to be at our groundbreaking. He'll already be in town to help Carrollton celebrate its fiftieth year as an incorporated city. And while he's here, he's agreed to come by and be with us too."

"That's great, Marcus. Listen, I can't talk right now, but let's get together tomorrow sometime to discuss the groundbreaking ceremony more. I have some ideas."

"Okay, David."

Texas governor John Connally indeed attended the groundbreaking, joining the Rosenbergs in marking the momentous occasion. In honor of his participation, Marcus and David asked the city of Carrollton if the new street where the plant was to be built could be named after the governor. The city obliged with the request, and Arrow became officially located on John Connally Drive.

David and Marcus Rosenberg going over the architectural plans of their new plant

Ten years prior to the move to Carrollton, Arrow was a two hundred thousand–dollar a year company, operating in five thousand square feet. In 1963, Arrow had a volume of more than ten million dollars and employed more than one hundred workers in the Carrollton plant alone. Arrow was on its way to becoming one of the nation's largest packagers and distributors of dried beans, processing more than 1.5 million pounds of beans that year. The company was also becoming a leading manufacturer of charcoal briquettes.

On November 30, 1964, Arrow filed another set of incorporation documents, this time, changing the company name to Arrow Food Products, Inc.

Chapter Two

With the exception of the folks living in the Midwest, most people didn't pay much attention to the weather in Nebraska. But Marcus did. Over the years, he would send trusted employees like his corporate group controller, Arnold Bier, up to Nebraska to keep close watch on what was happening in the region. If the weather was good and a bumper crop of beans was anticipated, Marcus would not take a position on the price of beans until they were harvested, cleaned, and ready to be delivered. But if an excessive amount of rain and hail fell in the Cornhusker state in a particular year, Marcus would take an early position on the bean crops. Because of the lessons he had learned in the Slovakian mills of his youth, Marcus understood the rules of supply and demand.

Going to the farmers well before the harvest, he might say, "Last year, you sold us forty thousand bushels. Today, I'll make a deal with you to buy another forty thousand at eighty cents per bushel when the crops come in."

And the farmers would make the deal with Marcus, because they didn't want to take a chance. They didn't know if the price was going to be $1.00, or $1.10, or 75¢ per bushel when it was time to sell their beans.

Arrow had an agreement with the US Department of Agriculture that, regardless of how much inventory the company had on hand, it would sell beans to its customers at the price set by the US Department of Agriculture on the day the order was placed. So if the price of beans was $1.00 on a particular day, and Safeway wanted to order some, Arrow would sell the beans to Safeway for $1.00 plus the packaging cost. But instead of waiting until January to lock in a price, Marcus likely would have taken an early position on those beans for something like 80¢ back in September, giving Arrow an edge over its competitors in the marketplace.

Marcus travelled the world looking for affordable suppliers of aluminum for Arrow's foil division. He would take Russ Fondren, his foil director for many years, on trips with him to destinations in Europe, South America, and China. Though they would always find quality product at good prices on these excursions, Marcus hoped to trim the cost of the materials even more without compromising on the grade of aluminum.

One of his goals was to work out a partnership with an overseas aluminum company so that Arrow could acquire the materials at a much lower price. Marcus tried on several occasions to find a supplier to partner with in Yugoslavia, Romania, and Turkey. In the end, however, this type of venture never worked out.

One day, Marcus was sitting in his office with Arrow's certified public accountant, Victor Trubitt. Deep purple and black wallpaper was paired with wood paneling. The curtains were closed as always. Marcus's desk was tidy and organized. Behind him on the credenza were a number of three-ring binders neatly lined up in a row. Inside those binders were Marcus's thoughts, ideas, and plans, all outlined and prioritized. Using his own system of organization, every aspect of Marcus's business and personal life was in those journals—projections, agendas, timetables. Marcus regularly revised the contents to ensure that everything was current and up-to-date with his rapid pace of daily life.

Marcus took a moment to light up a cigarette. Other than the banker's light on his desk and the glow from the burning cigarette, the room was dark. Slowly exhaling a drag from his cigarette, Marcus began to speak. Just then, the phone rang.

"Excuse me for a moment, Victor," he said. "Hello," Marcus said as he picked up the receiver. He paused. "Yes, yes, I understand. Okay, I would like to purchase the pepper at the price we discussed yesterday. And the delivery to our door will be two weeks from tomorrow? Yes, good. Okay, just send me the papers and I'll sign them. Thank you very much."

When Marcus hung up the phone, he looked at Victor.

"You know that boatload of pepper I told you about yesterday?" he asked. "The one coming from India? I just purchased it."

"Geez, Marcus," Victor exclaimed. "You haven't even seen the pepper! You don't know anything about it! How can you go buy a boatload of pepper you know nothing about?"

"Victor, don't worry. It will be fine," Marcus said.

And in general, the decisions Marcus made for Arrow were fine—better than fine. Not everything ended up as Marcus may have hoped, but his understanding of market trends and his skills for buying high-quality product at very low prices contributed to the growth of Arrow's profits year after year.

In the 1960s, Marcus took a big step toward trimming the production costs of processing beans. Initially, Arrow was purchasing large rolls of plastic to bag the beans. Plastic was not inexpensive, especially in substantial quantities, and Marcus asked himself why he was paying for it when he could just as well produce it himself. He starting looking into what would be involved in manufacturing plastic in-house at Arrow.

After calling on several people to give him quotes on plastic-making machines, Marcus was having a hard time getting anyone to take him seriously. He finally pressed one salesman, who told Marcus that it was a very complicated process and, frankly, he didn't think Marcus had the ability to implement it.

Marcus looked the salesman in the eye and told him, "I don't need you to tell me I can't do it. I need you to tell me *how* I can do it."

Marcus did figure out how to produce and print his own plastic bags, and the cost savings to Arrow were substantial over time.

Not long after that, Marcus questioned the method of packaging rice. All rice at that time was packed in polypropylene, a crinkly plastic derivative that was much more expensive than regular plastic. Marcus wondered why they did not just pack the rice in the same plastic they used to pack the beans. He told the people on the production line to change the rice packaging to the less costly bags.

Everything seemed to be going well for a while until the ink writing on the outside of the rice bags started smearing. This had never happened with the old packaging, so why was it happening now? And why wasn't it happening with the beans?

After doing some research, Marcus discovered that rice has natural oils. These oils migrated through the regular plastic, loosened up the ink, and caused it to smear. But instead of reverting back to the more costly polypropylene, Marcus instead ordered the production line to run two layers of plastic to create the new rice bags. This approach was still less expensive than the polypropylene and ended up solving the problem—the rice oils and the ink never met again. Once this method of packaging was perfected, the entire rice packing industry followed Marcus's techniques to save money.

The changes in the rice packaging worked well for Marcus, but Arrow was not successful in all of its endeavors. Several products along the way simply did not develop as planned. For example, at one point Arrow tried to sell dog food. As it turned out, the product was especially susceptible to insects and infestation, which did not bode well for the other food products Arrow was storing and selling. Another time, Arrow carried a nonalcoholic beer. That was not profitable for them, nor was the dried fruit they marketed.

Just before freeze-dried coffee was introduced to the marketplace, Arrow tried its hand at packaging instant coffee. A special coffee room was set up at the plant, and the key element for productive packaging was to keep the coffee flowing. This entailed maintaining near-zero humidity in the room. Dehumidifiers were set up at the plant, but somehow, Arrow never completely mastered the process. Everything in the room had coffee on it. Small brown blobs were ever-present on the machinery, the ladders, the floor, the packaged product itself. Over time, the small blobs grew into bigger blobs. Eventually, Arrow ceased its coffee packaging production and hauled the processing equipment upstairs to its eternal resting place in an out-of-the-way storage room.

While some of their projects were not lucrative, Marcus and David were always innovative, and in the end, achieved their goals far more often than not.

In the 1970s, the volume of beans coming and going through the doors of Arrow grew exponentially. Cutting costs on packaging was helpful to the company, but Marcus sought even more dramatic changes in production to further improve profitability.

Beans were delivered to Arrow from bean producers in one hundred-pound burlap bags. When the product arrived by train to the plant, someone had to cut open the bags and dump the beans out for storage until processing time. So Marcus looked for ways to reduce manual handling in the system.

His first idea was to explore purchasing a bean-producing facility in Nebraska. Pinto beans and great northern beans were grown primarily in that part of the country, and a large bean elevator was for sale. Marcus and his chief financial officer (CFO) at the time, Lionel Goldstein, travelled to Nebraska in the dead of winter to check it out. After looking over the property and crawling up and down the silos, Marcus decided it would be a very good operation to purchase. Not only was the plant one of the larger handlers of beans in the country, but if the Rosenbergs owned it, they could decide how to ship the beans to Dallas.

Upon acquiring the bean elevator, Marcus changed the shipping process at the plant such that beans were no longer packed in burlap bags. Instead, they were dumped directly into railcars—each car had the capacity to hold two hundred thousand pounds—and sent to Dallas.

The second step in improving the efficiency of processing beans was to modify the way the beans were unloaded from the trains. Marcus conceptualized an idea that entailed taking bean-filled railcars and emptying their contents directly into storage bins with no human intervention. This vision led to a revolutionary new delivery system.

A special gravity-flow elevator facility was built where the railroad tracks reached Arrow's plant. This facility enabled a railway car to be placed above an opening in the ground through which the contents of the railcar could be dumped down onto a conveyer that took the beans and automatically stored them in two thousand–pound metal bins. Stamped with the date of arrival, these bins were then moved by forklift and stacked in the warehouse until the beans were needed for processing.

Beans being delivered to Arrow

One of Arrow's warehouses

No other plant in the country had a system like this in place. Marcus's inventiveness, paired with his resolve to implement new ideas, again put Arrow ahead of its competitors.

Chapter Three

❧

$\mathcal{D}$avid and Marcus found their niche not only in selling beans but also in manufacturing private label products. Grocery stores could have their own company brand names and logos printed on the containers of all Arrow products—from beans to rice, paper plates to popcorn, pepper to foil, whatever items Arrow was manufacturing.

David's customer base allowed him to see more and more opportunities in the marketplace, and as Arrow's product offerings grew, so did the number of private labels. Arrow's list of customers came to include almost all of the top grocery store chains at the time—Tom Thumb, Food Club, Safeway, Shop Rite, Topco, Fleming Food, Kroger, A&P, and Affiliated. Selling to companies across the country, Arrow had as many as nine hundred private labels at its peak.

Originally, Arrow ran its production lines according to customer orders as they came in. For example, if a customer wanted twenty-four two-pound bags of black beans, Arrow would run the request and then move on to the next customer order, which might have been for forty-eight one-pound bags of split peas. Changes in product and packaging such as these required many interruptions in the flow of operation. More often than not, the production runs were very short and very expensive. Marcus saw this as another shortcoming and inefficiency that needed to be corrected. It was clear that the more units produced without making a change on

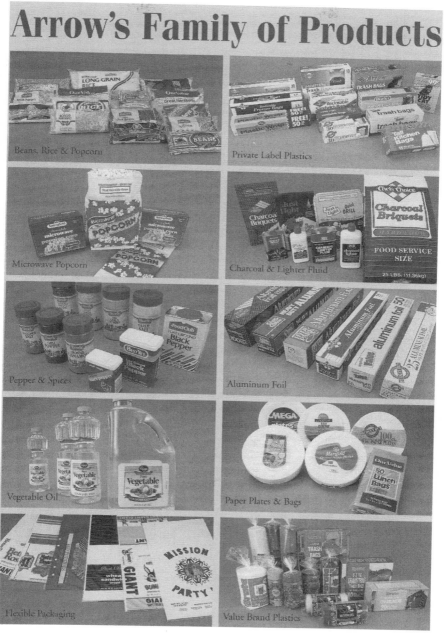

Company brochure of Arrow's offerings

the production line resulted in a lower cost per unit. But how could this be done if the customer ordered only a certain amount?

Comfortable that its customer base was largely stable and reliable, Arrow began applying the principle of executing longer runs, producing more than the customer ordered and storing the overage for future transactions. The cost benefit of these changes was quickly seen, but Arrow's need for additional storage space grew much more rapidly as well. As a result, the concept of forward warehouses came into being.

Arrow distribution trucks

Forward warehouses were storage facilities set up close to major delivery points, used when Arrow overproduced private-label product for a particular customer. The extra product was stored in these warehouses and delivered when a later order came in. Not only did this ease some of the demand for additional storage at Arrow's corporate headquarters, but it also cut customer delivery lead times and allowed more flexibility in ordering. In addition, customers were able to trim their own inventory cost of storing extra product, because Arrow was doing it for them. Figuring out the optimal balance between inventory levels and customer lead times was initially a challenge for Arrow, but they became quite adept at it.

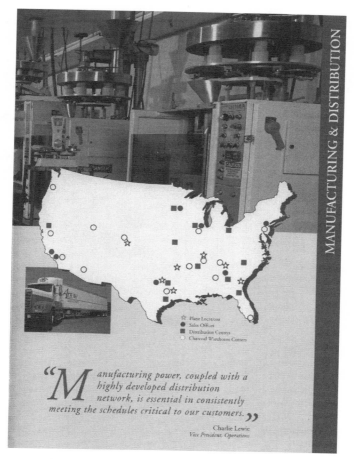

Arrow manufacturing and distribution brochure

To meet the increased demand of clients, Arrow established forward warehouses all across the country, from Portland, Oregon, to Miami, Florida. The bottom lines for both Arrow and its customers benefitted greatly from the arrangement.

The forward warehouses did help with storage needs at Arrow overall, but they did not totally eliminate the problem. As Arrow's business continued to grow, so did its need to store additional product, especially at the facility in Carrollton. More warehouses were added, but the company never quite seemed to have enough space.

Marcus was taking one of his traditional Sunday morning walks around the plant, accompanied on this particular day by Lionel Goldstein, Arrow's CFO at the time. The topic of the company's ongoing storage challenges came up. Arrow was in the process of building another warehouse, this one designed to be two hundred thousand square feet. Marcus wanted to see how this facility could be set up differently somehow to maximize the potential of all the new square footage.

Lionel told Marcus about a new type of forklift he had come across recently. This forklift was different; it could turn on a dime and navigate

Narrow aisle forklift at Arrow

much narrower aisles—half the width required by traditional forklifts. That was all Marcus needed to hear. He decided to purchase some of the newfangled forklifts, and with that, the interior of the new warehouse was designed with narrower, taller aisles. As a result, the building's storage capacity increased greatly from its original plans.

Chapter Four

❧

S porting long, thick black hair and a fu manchu mustache, Charlie Lewie was working up a sweat. Unloading boxes of furniture from freight trucks was hard work, but doing so in the hot Texas summer in an unair-conditioned warehouse was almost too much to bear, even for this distinguished war veteran. Recently returned from Vietnam, where he served as a sniper, Charlie was working at Falcon Furniture in Carrollton, Texas. This job was just something to do while he transitioned back into civilian life after his long tour of duty.

On his way into work one day in October 1970, Charlie noticed a "Help Wanted" sign across the street at a large industrial complex for a company named Arrow. Charlie had been curious about this company, even wondering what went on on the sprawling property. Because he was tired of his dead-end job at the furniture store, Charlie walked over to see what kind of help Arrow might need.

After locating the human resources department, he asked if any jobs were available. Charlie was told that, in two weeks, a position in quality control would be opening up. Charlie had an interview with the manager of that department, Gerry Reisberg. Impressed with Charlie, Gerry offered him a job and then walked him around the facility.

Charlie was shown the pepper room, where long plastic curtain strips at the doorway protected those on the outside from the effects of breathing in too much of the zesty spice. Next Charlie saw where the aluminum foil was processed. Huge rolls of aluminum ran through a series of machines that cut the foil at the appropriate lengths—seventy-five feet, two hundred feet, whatever was specified by the customer whose order was being processed—and then packaged in the customer's store-branded boxes.

Finally, Charlie made it to the bean-processing plant. He saw there a never-ending assembly line of beans running across high-speed conveyer belts and being sorted, shaken, cleaned, filtered, and ultimately packaged.

Never having seen anything like it in his life, Charlie was very impressed. He looked around at everything in front of him, taking it all in.

Arrow foil production line

Then he saw something that struck him as odd. On the floor of the bean plant, a distinguished man wearing suit pants and a white shirt was sweeping the floor with a push broom. He seemed out of place. Charlie looked over at Gerry and asked who this person was.

"Oh," Gerry said, "that's Marcus Rosenberg. He's the president of the company."

Charlie was taken aback, thinking to himself that if the president of this massive operation was down on the floor sweeping up, then this was probably a person who would not ask Charlie to do something he would not do himself. Seeing Marcus in that light inspired Charlie, and he accepted the job offer, becoming Arrow's two hundredth employee. Charlie began his career as a quality control inspector, which was a good place to start, because it required learning about and working in all the departments.

Every morning, Marcus would begin his day by walking the floor. He would go everywhere—in the lines, in the back, up in front. He would say hello to everyone. If he saw some refuse on the floor, he'd pick it up and put it in the trash can. These morning walks set the tone with Arrow's employees who understood that Marcus was as much a part of the operation as they were. He didn't sit in his office all day with the door closed. Marcus was hands-on and tuned in to what was going on in the plant.

It was on these morning walks that Charlie first had the opportunity to get to know and work with Marcus.

"Good morning, Marcus," Charlie would say. All employees called Marcus by his first name, even hourly employees like Charlie.

"Good morning, Charlie," Marcus would respond. "How's everything looking for today?"

Knowing that good quality and high standards were of great importance at Arrow, Charlie might say, "Well, I'm not sure about the new batch of beans that came in. I'm concerned they may have some kind of mold on them."

And Marcus would typically respond, "Okay, let's go up to the top of the railcar and take a look at the beans. Then we'll see what we should do with them."

One morning, Marcus pointed over to the inventory board. Black-eyed peas, split peas, black beans, northern beans, great pinto beans, short rice, long rice, popcorn, and more were stored in huge silos. A large board with various magnetic markers was used on the floor to indicate inventory levels of all the products.

Marcus asked Charlie, "What's happening with the black beans? Why is the marker at the same place as yesterday? Are we not using those beans?"

"Oh yes, we're using the black beans," Charlie said. "I'm sorry, Marcus, I forgot to move the marker."

"Oh, that's okay, Charlie. I just wanted to make sure," Marcus said.

After working for a while at Arrow, Charlie told Marcus that he was being pressured by his father to go to college. His father was teaching at the University of Texas at Arlington, and Charlie had access to the GI bill because he had served in the army. Tuition costs weren't a problem for attending college, but Charlie didn't want to take a four-year break from Arrow. He wanted to stay and learn as much as he could.

"Look at me, Charlie," Marcus said. "I don't have an expensive education. In fact, I didn't even go to high school. I only went to school through eighth grade. But I worked hard, Charlie, and I learned what I needed. You can do it too. I will teach you everything you need to know."

So Charlie skipped the classroom education and opted to continue acquiring practical experience in the field. He quickly rose from his position as quality inspector to quality supervisor and then to manager of the department. Later, Charlie became a production coordinator, scheduling operations for all the departments, a particularly complicated task since all planning and coordinating was done by hand at that time. Charlie continued learning about the company by becoming a supervisor in the foil department and then the division manager over the bean, pepper, and charcoal lighter areas.

Around 1976, Marcus asked Charlie if he would go to La Vergne, Tennessee, just outside of Nashville, to run Arrow's bean-processing plant there. Arrow had set up a plant in Tennessee because the largest concentration of bean-eaters in the country was on the east coast. Having bean-processing plants in both the Dallas and Nashville areas assured the greatest efficiencies in delivering product to Arrow's customers.

Charlie saw this as a good opportunity to grow professionally and agreed to go. When he first began working in La Vergne, Marcus visited him frequently, helping him make decisions on which equipment to purchase, logistical issues, and so forth. On one of these visits, Marcus went with Charlie to see his new home in Smyrna.

Charlie loved this home and had spoken about it quite a bit to Marcus. The house sat on almost one acre of land, and while it wasn't far from the bean plant, it had the feel of being out in the country. When Marcus got there, he saw Charlie's two-year-old son playing in the front yard. Concerned that the toddler might wander out into the road, Marcus told Charlie to have Sears come out and put a fence all the way around so that the little boy couldn't get out. Charlie thought Marcus was kidding, but when Marcus repeated himself, Charlie realized he was serious. Charlie called Sears to put up the fence, and Marcus covered the cost. Charlie could not believe that Marcus would care that much; as a result of this experience, Charlie's loyalty to Arrow grew even deeper.

After the first couple of years, once he became comfortable that Charlie was running the plant well, Marcus's visits to La Vergne slowed to once a year.

Charlie worked in La Vergne for over six years. Then he trained his replacement plant manager and moved back to Dallas to become the vice president of operations at Arrow.

Charlie Lewie, early 1990s

Chapter Five

*I*n the late 1960s and early 1970s, after Arrow had become a very profitable company, Marcus and David decided to go through the process of going public. Victor Trubitt went to work for the company to help develop the prospectus and see that Arrow's statements became certified. Lionel Goldstein became involved in consolidating all of Arrow's divisions—each individual charcoal plant, plus Arrow Foods, and the various real estate holdings—into one entity. Alexander Grant & Co., one of the nation's largest accounting firms, was also engaged to assist with the due diligence, looking at audit and tax implication issues. Arrow spent a large amount of money—around $250,000—on attorneys, accountants, printers, and others in the effort to become a publicly held company.

The day before Arrow was to go public, the underwriting firm lowered the offering price, blaming the change on market conditions. Marcus was incensed and refused to accept the new pricing. Feeling misled by the underwriting company, he shut down the process. Many senior employees in the company were equally disappointed that the deal fell through; they were set to be given shares of the company and become owners of Arrow.

Because of all the consolidation that resulted from this effort, Arrow incorporated once more in June 1972, this time officially changing the company name to Arrow Industries.

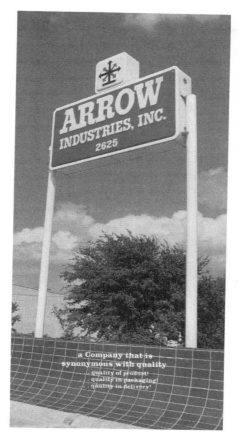

Arrow's front entrance in Carrollton

In the mid-1980s, Arrow again went through the exercise of going public, and again the process broke down. At that time, the markets were very volatile, and Marcus felt they would have been selling at too low of a price.

In the end, Arrow remained a privately held company, and perhaps that was the way it was meant to be. Marcus and David had been self-employed, independent thinkers all their lives. Becoming a publicly traded company would have meant they would have to report to someone, be overseen by a board, which may or may not have agreed with the Rosenberg brothers' strategies for running the business. Neither Marcus nor David liked to be forced into anything.

Chapter Six

❦

*I*n 1967, when Gregg Hanson began working at Arrow, he started at the bottom of the ladder. Working the second shift from four thirty p.m. to one a.m., the long-haired college student spent his time unloading aluminum from delivery crates. Gregg liked the job, because it fit his lifestyle while in college, plus it paid ten cents more per hour than the day shift did. Just two weeks later, he was moved to the position of machine operator, and his salary increased to $2.20 per hour. Another eight months passed by, and Gregg was promoted to foreman, which bumped his salary up to $2.75 per hour. In less than a year, this college student moved from unloading crates to a management position in the foil division at Arrow. As a result, he changed his college major from art to business management.

When he moved into management, Gregg had the opportunity to work directly with Marcus. Together they would discuss budgeting and other issues concerning foil production. Over time, Gregg became the director of operations for both the aluminum foil and paper plate product lines. Even though he wasn't a Rosenberg family member, Gregg felt very much part of the Arrow family, part of something that was really growing.

Gregg saw that the Rosenbergs cared about their employees, especially those who had been around for some time and proven themselves to be loyal to the company. If employees needed help buying a refrigerator or were short on cash, they knew the Rosenbergs could be counted on to help.

When workers clocked in extra overtime, they were rewarded by Marcus or David with a ten-dollar bill or a six-pack of beer. The employees were entrusted as caretakers of the business, and the Rosenbergs felt a strong sense of responsibility to watch over them.

Just before Gregg got married, Marcus came up to him, tucked two crisp one hundred–dollar bills in his shirt pocket, and said, "Congratulations on getting married, Gregg. Marriage makes men better."

One day, Marcus and Gregg were going through a number of invoices, because they had discovered some discrepancies in pricing from one particular supplier, a paper mill in southern Texas. According to the invoices, Arrow owed this mill more money than they had originally estimated. It seemed that, somewhere along the way, the agreed-upon rates had been changed by the supplier. Marcus was not happy about paying extra money, because he believed the mill had not been transparent about the price increase. To resolve the issue, Marcus summoned the vice president of the mill and the mill's salesman up to Dallas.

The two visitors were sitting in the conference room when Marcus walked in with a stack of invoices at least eighteen inches high. With a frown, he slammed the invoices on the table. In his deep, raspy voice, he slowly said, "You need to tell me and Gregg which of these invoices are right, and you need to tell us which ones are wrong. We will sit here all afternoon with you, but you need to go through invoice by invoice and tell us which ones were before you raised the price, and which ones were after you raised the price. You also need to tell us how much inventory you were holding of the product at the old price, and how much of the new product you ran. Because we can't figure it out."

"You're obviously smarter than we are," Marcus continued. "You say we owe something different than what we figured out based on the pricing we agreed upon together. So you need to show us why we owe you this extra money."

The vice president and the salesman looked at each other and then went into the corner to talk. When they came back, the vice president asked, "Mr. Rosenberg, how much do you think you owe us?"

Marcus and Gregg went into another corner to talk. They came back with a number they believed was fair.

The two men from the mill agreed with the figure, shook hands with Marcus and Gregg, and told them that they appreciated their business.

After they left, Marcus turned to Gregg and said, "Sometimes you have to put the burden of proof on them. You don't have to prove everything. Let them prove it to you."

Still astounded by the exchange, Gregg agreed with the wisdom of Marcus's strategy.

Chapter Seven

❦

*M*arcus drove his new Lincoln Town Car into the parking lot at the Columbian Club just down the road from Arrow. The country club was established in the late 1800s by a group of Dallas Jewish men who had been excluded from joining non-Jewish country clubs in the city. In the late 1950s, the Columbian Club moved out to Carrollton, very close to where Arrow's corporate headquarters would be located. The property was beautiful with its lush two hundred acres, featuring an eighteen-hole golf course, a swimming pool, tennis courts, and a picturesque lake. In the club was a small restaurant where Marcus frequently ate lunch with friends and fellow employees. His favorite dish was the Farmer Salad, which consisted of cottage cheese and vegetables. The Columbian Club also had several large rooms used for all sorts of social events. On this night, the club was hosting Arrow's annual formal holiday party.

As they pulled up to the valet parking, Marcus and Ann got out of the car. Arnold Bier, Arrow's corporate group comptroller, saw him and with a wink said, "Nice car, Marcus!"

"Eh, old man car," Marcus said with a smile. Then he let out his signature giggle, "Hee hee hee …"

Arnold caught up with Marcus inside and said, "Can you believe it, Marcus? Prime rate just hit eighteen percent! I don't know how I'm ever going to get that new house now."

"I'll tell you what, Arnold," Marcus said. "If that Jimmy Carter were the CEO of a company, I'd fire him!"

Marcus was happy and looking forward to the evening ahead. Every year, he went around the room, shaking hands and talking with everyone. He'd share a drink and have his picture taken with many of his employees.

Marcus and Ann Rosenberg visiting with employees at the annual holiday party

All the office staff and their spouses were there, as were any other employees who had worked at the company for ten years or more. The spread of food was lavish and delicious, and the music and dancing went on well into the night. People were dressed in their Sunday best, and recognition awards were given out to those employees who had shined during the year.

Arrow also hosted an annual picnic in the springtime for all employees and their families. At Sandy Lake Park, families could enjoy swimming, amusement rides, miniature golf, and paddle boats on the lake. Arrow served a barbecue lunch to everyone, in later years numbering more than several thousand people. Marcus told the employees to bring their whole families. Spouses and children would be there, and sometimes aunts, uncles, and cousins as well. Arrow raffled off TVs, radios, and other goodies. Everyone had an enjoyable time. Despite the crowds, Marcus could be easily found—he was the one wearing a suit and tennis shoes.

Arrow was run by a family and had a family feel to it. Employees tended to stay there a very long time. The two original employees, Eloisa and Frances Carrasco, worked for many decades at Arrow. Some employees left—sometimes to relocate, sometimes for more money—but often, they returned to Arrow and were welcomed back with open arms. Some employees thought about leaving but enjoyed the atmosphere at the company so much that they stayed on.

Arrow hosted golf and tennis tournaments and had softball teams that played in Carrollton's leagues

Marcus Rosenberg looking over a twenty-year service award for employee Charlie Lewie in December 1990; Karen Lewie is seated next to her husband.

as well. A bimonthly newsletter, first called *Arrow Aims* (in the 1970s) and then *Arrow Spirit* (in the 1980s and onward) was sent out to keep employees in touch with who was celebrating birthdays and anniversaries, who was having babies, who had reached milestones in service, and what exciting and relevant happenings were taking place at the company.

Employees could also take part in the company's profit-sharing plan. And those who really excelled in job performance might be sent on cruises to exotic places like Australia. In terms of employee recognition, Arrow was very progressive for its time.

～～*～*～*～*～*～*

Mike Campbell moved to Dallas in 1983 right out of college. His first job was processing claims at a life insurance company. After a year of doing that type of work, he saw an advertisement for a position at Arrow dealing with benefits. Because he had taken many college courses on benefits handling, Mike decided to look into the opportunity. When he sent in the necessary information to Arrow, he got a call from Marcus to come in and talk about the position. After Marcus covered a few questions, he offered the job to Mike. Mike accepted.

One of the reasons Marcus hired Mike was because of his experience in processing claims. Marcus was very interested in Arrow becoming self-insured. He wanted the company to run a self-funded medical program in which Arrow would process the claims and negotiate discounts with hospitals and providers—basically everything a third-party provider would do. Marcus believed that running the insurance in-house instead of paying a third-party administrator or insurance company would dramatically cut down on costs. Initially, Mike wasn't sure that the numbers would work out that way, but after analyzing the company's claim dollars compared to premiums being paid out, he determined that, sure enough, Marcus was correct in his assessment.

With only one year of work experience under his belt, Mike was given the responsibility of building a benefits department at Arrow. Feeling very fortunate for the opportunity, Mike began to set up the in-house systems required to handle Arrow's health insurance needs. After doing much research, he selected a software package that could be used to adjudicate the claims and cut the checks. Marcus gave Mike the leeway to make mistakes along the way and learn from them. For this, Mike was grateful.

Marcus indeed gave Mike latitude, but he didn't just sit off to the side, waiting for this new insurance program to take hold. Not only was he in very close touch with Mike, but Marcus actually signed every single one of the claims checks himself before each was mailed to an employee.

This oversight resembled another practice he had followed since the company had been established. Every Friday afternoon, Marcus packed the week's payable invoices in a worn-out box and took them home. Over the weekend, he went through the invoices one by one, making sure he knew exactly what was being purchased and how much was being paid out by the company. No check was ever cut by the accounts payable department unless Marcus himself approved the expense with his legendary "MR" stamp at the bottom of the invoice. Though he was president of a very large corporation, Marcus still involved himself intrinsically in the day-to-day business, always keeping his finger on the pulse.

Arrow ran its medical insurance in-house for five years. As the company opened additional plants and locations around the country, the number of employees grew and negotiating discounts in Dallas and in states such as Arkansas and Tennessee became more difficult. When the process stopped paying for itself, Arrow went back to using a third-party administrator for their PPO networks and processing the claims. However, the Rosenbergs' company continued to be self-funded.

Workers compensation was another area that Arrow endeavored to handle in-house. At the time, the state of Texas allowed companies to drop out of the state worker compensation program and either be self-funded or have no coverage at all. More than willing to be a guinea pig, Marcus positioned Arrow as one of the very first businesses in Texas to opt out of this coverage. If someone was injured on the job, Arrow made sure the bills got paid and the employee was compensated. If an injured employee hired an attorney, then Manny, in his role as one of Arrow's legal counselors, would get involved and work out some sort of settlement that was amenable to both the employee and to Arrow. Arrow saved hundreds of thousands of dollars in insurance premiums. Several years later, when changes were made to Texas' worker compensation system, it became more feasible to opt back into the program.

While self-funding continued to be a big cost saver for Arrow, Marcus sought to further the savings by introducing an incentive program that was run in each division—for example, charcoal, plastics, aluminum foil. If no claims were filed for a particular month, a $100 safety bonus was given to each employee in the division. The bonus escalated as well, and if a division went without a claim for a quarter, the payoff was $250 per employee. Two consecutive quarters without a reported injury resulted in a $500 bonus. When safety milestones were reached, bonuses were presented at the company-sponsored luncheons where employees received their awards.

If however, anyone filed a claim, the entire division would lose out on the bonus. These bonuses were a huge incentive, especially for hourly employees working on the production lines. Consequently, light injuries did not typically get reported. The idea of everyone in a department losing a collective bonus because one employee had gotten hurt simply did not sit well, so much so, that a slightly morbid joke was told at Arrow:

"Hey, did you hear Joe's leg got cut off in the plant the other day?"

"No, that's awful! How's he doing?"

"Well, he didn't file a claim, and he's still coming into work."

"Why's that?"

"Well, he was so scared about what his coworkers would do if they lost their bonus, he figured it was a lot easier to just pretend it never happened."

"Good for Joe!"

"Good for his coworkers!"

Jokes aside, Marcus's innovative spirit propelled him to become a pioneer in industry. No one was self-insured at that time, nor did anyone have an incentive program like Arrow's in place.

In the mid- to late 1980s, an Arrow employee was crushed to death in a production machine. The crushed worker was represented by one of the premier personal injury law firms in Dallas, considered among the best in the state of Texas. The death was fully covered by the comprehensive general liability insurance held by Arrow, but the law firm wanted a very large settlement. Therefore, the lawyers looked for a way to pressure Marcus and others at Arrow so that they in turn would pressure the insurance company. Their tactic was to bring a claim against Marcus individually, using a strategy called "piercing the corporate veil." They aimed to prove that the corporation was a shield for Marcus, with him treating the corporation like his own, writing personal checks, and so on.

To Richard Rohan, a Harvard law graduate and Manny's son, this tactic was ridiculous. The allegations were completely unfounded, and legally, an individual is not liable for the debts of a corporation in a situation such as this. The law firm was using this approach solely to pressure Arrow and the insurance company into a larger settlement.

After Marcus was named, the plaintiff's law firm wanted to take his deposition to discover how he treated the company as well as determine all sorts of other financial information. They had a punitive damages claim against Marcus, and when such a case is asserted, the net worth of the individual can be discovered in order to determine an appropriate amount of punitive damages to pay. So at Marcus's deposition, he was asked a number of questions about his net worth. Marcus refused to answer anything, saying that he had constitutional rights. However, he did talk at length about his side of the story, expounding point by point. Frustrated with Marcus's lack of cooperation, the law firm filed a motion asking that the court compel Marcus to answer the questions.

The presiding judge was an older gentleman who, in the course of the case, became charmed by Marcus. Everything about Marcus's story resonated with him, as it did with many people. Here is Marcus, a man from the old country who went through much hardship and came out on the other side very successful and accomplished. In the end, Marcus prevailed in that he did not have to answer the questions about his net worth.

The lawsuit was resolved by the insurance company paying a lot of money to the deceased employee's family and to their attorney.

That was how Richard had figured it would be resolved. He had never thought anything was ever going to be paid by Arrow or Marcus, but the lawyers still tried to force him to sit down and disclose his personal information. Marcus didn't give in, and by fighting on principle, he came out on top.

Chapter Eight

All of Marcus's children at one point or another worked at Arrow. Helen was the human resources manager for a while. Margot was a customer service representative. Lizzy helped with the planning of company picnics and parties. Sheri was employed briefly in accounts payable. And they all had the opportunity to work summers at the plant and go in with Marcus on Sunday mornings.

One Fourth of July weekend, some extra filing needed to be done, so Lizzy brought the work home with her and finished it. When she woke up in the morning, she found a one hundred–dollar bill and a note of thanks from her father saying:

> Dear Liz,
> In appreciation for a job well done into the late hours.
> Here's $100—Have a ball!

At the age of seven, Steven began going to Arrow with his father. When he was nine, he was in the factory working on equipment. By the age of twelve, Steven could be found in the machine shop of the plant, building parts for various pieces of machinery. And when he was sixteen, he was in the plant making business decisions on logistics, shipping, and so on. He even spent a summer at the plant near Nashville. Steven's natural talents and genuine interest in the company enabled him to get to know the business and the operations of Arrow very well.

In the early 1980s, Steven attended New York University and was working toward a degree in finance. During Steven's senior year of college, Marcus went to Scranton, Pennsylvania, to visit the American Can Liners manufacturing facility.

American Can Liners was auctioning off all of its equipment, and Marcus was interested in purchasing some printing presses. At the time, Arrow was operating a number of four-color presses to print on polyethylene plastic used for bean, rice, and popcorn packaging. Marcus was looking to upgrade to more sophisticated machinery and went to Scranton to see three specific printing presses. Each machine had a sign posted with the press' value and expected selling price. After seeing these, Marcus walked around the rest of the plant to look over the other available equipment. He quickly calculated that he could probably buy the whole operation for close to what he had originally been prepared to pay for the three printing presses.

Marcus approached the auctioneer and said, "I'd like to make an offer to buy all the equipment in the plant here." Marcus told him the amount he was willing to pay.

"I'm sorry, sir," the auctioneer said. "This is an auction. We're not selling the whole plant in its entirety."

"Listen," Marcus said, "why don't you call the owner and tell him that you have someone here willing to pay for the whole plant outright. Tell him what I'm offering and see what he says."

The auctioneer reluctantly did as Marcus told him, and to his surprise, the owner was very interested. Thirty minutes before the auction even started, Marcus became the owner of twenty truckloads of machinery. All the other businessmen who had travelled to Scranton that day to purchase equipment at the auction went home empty-handed.

Afterward, Marcus got on the phone and called Steven in New York.

"Steven, I'm in Pennsylvania. I just purchased the American Can Liners plant in Scranton. There's twenty trucks' worth of machinery here.

The plant is still in operation, and I want you to come down to look at it and see what you think."

"Are you serious?" Steven asked. "That equipment is much more sophisticated than what we're using at Arrow."

"Well, I bought it anyway, and we're going to move it to Dallas in the summer."

Arrow waited six months to transfer the equipment down to its corporate plant. During this window of time, not only had the former owners in Scranton not maintained the equipment properly, but parts of machines had been removed, new motors had been replaced with old ones, and so on. Not realizing what had happened at the time, Arrow eventually discovered that what they had purchased was not what they had received. Two consultants were brought in to set up the equipment at the Garden Brook plant, which was located across the street from the Arrow headquarters in Carrollton.

That same summer, Steven graduated from college and got married. He also began working at Arrow full-time. In the beginning, Steven had no involvement with the equipment from Scranton. Instead, Marcus had Steven by his side, shadowing him throughout the day so that Steven could learn what his father did at Arrow.

In the meantime, the reassembling of the Scranton equipment was not going well. After six or seven months, Marcus was just about ready to give up on the project and sell off what he could. Steven went to Marcus and asked if he would give him twelve months to try his hand at getting the equipment to work. Knowing Steven's mechanical skills and technical abilities, Marcus agreed to the proposal, and the younger Rosenberg set out to see what he could do. The equipment was not in good shape at all, but Steven did manage to get it up and running. Plastic bags began being produced, and some customers started buying the product.

Steven proved he could do something with very little, and when he went to Marcus with a request to purchase some newer equipment, Marcus gave his blessing.

Arrow's Garden Brook plant began to grow. The number of production lines expanded, as did the types of products. The flexible packaging offerings came to include bread bags; ice cube bags; bakery bags; potato bags; carrot bags; and all shapes, colors, and sizes of trash bags. For food product bags, Arrow worked with each customer on specific, individualized design, offering up to eight colors per imprinted label.

Arrow graphic design artist

The operation was impressive. Railcars would come in carrying resin, small clear pellets of polyethylene. The resin was stored in silos, each holding more than two hundred thousand pounds, until the resin was ready to be processed into bags. During processing, the resin was fed from a hopper into the barrel of an extruder. Color additives were poured in depending on the type of plastic being extruded—orange was for highway trash bags; red was for hospital bags; blue was for recycling. Scented resin was for bathroom trash can liners. Next, the resin was melted at four hundred to 450 degrees Fahrenheit until it reached the consistency of syrup. Then it travelled into a big machine where cool air was blown in,

" The successful application of highly advanced and cost efficient technologies, combined with intelligent choices in vertical integration into component manufacturing, assures Arrow's position as a top quality, low cost manufacturer. "

John Gielow
Vice Presidents, Sales & Marketing
Flexible Packing Division

Richard Meredith
Vice President and General Manager
Flexible Packing Division

Arrow flexible packaging brochure

causing a huge bubble of plastic to shoot up some thirty to forty feet in the air before collapsing and being fashioned into the desired shape and size. Stopping and starting these machines was a long, complicated process, so the extrusion lines ran twenty-four hours a day, seven days a week.

Arrow plastics production line

* ～ * ～ * ～ * ～ * ～ * ～ * ～ * ～ *

Michael Conway, previously a comptroller at Otis Engineering, was brought into Arrow as the CFO in 1984. When he began his new job, Michael learned that the work done at Arrow was completely different than the work done in the oil field manufacturing industry. Arrow's business was based on using high volumes of material for which acquisition was oftentimes determined by erratic market conditions. Plus, the profit was very low per unit—only a penny or two—so any added cost could jeopardize the bottom line. Such low profit margins required very high volumes of sales. Not only did Michael come to understand the value of trimming a cent or two off of production costs, but he also came to greatly appreciate Marcus's ability to run the production lines so efficiently and effectively.

One day, Michael went to Marcus's office to talk about the mounting equipment costs in the extrusion division. Each additional extrusion line was a million-dollar investment. A new color press cost $1.5 million.

As Michael and Marcus began to talk, Steven walked in. Marcus looked up and said, "You know, the problem here is that Steven's father is a rich man."

Despite this quip, whenever Steven requested new equipment, Marcus agreed to purchase it; not only did his son continue to show a return on investment, but the returns were realized in a reasonable amount of time. In less than ten years, the plastics division and its business grew from three extrusion lines to more than twenty.

Arrow plastics production line

⁓⁓*⁓*⁓*⁓*⁓*⁓*⁓*

Steven could see how computers were affecting business and the broader world. While Marcus installed some extraordinary systems at Arrow, he did not keep up with the growth of computers and was not tuned in to the benefits that they could offer companies. After Steven explained how computerization would help Arrow become more efficient and streamlined, Marcus allowed Steven to purchase computers for the business side of the operation. The cost of investment was steep, but modernizing the company was critical at the time. Steven changed Arrow very quickly in this regard, and while some risk was inevitable, that risk was mitigated because the upgrades allowed the company to grow even faster.

Once when Steven was set to go out of town on a business trip, one of his employees, Jozef Levi, asked to borrow Steven's computer while he was away. Jozef had been brought into Arrow as a management trainee. With two degrees (industrial engineering and business management) he was the perfect candidate for the program, which was designed to rotate trainees around to all different areas of the company, wherever a need within management was determined. Jozef started in plastics, where he worked for a few months. He asked to use Steven's computer because he wanted to modernize the way scheduling, supply ordering, and other tasks were executed in the plastics area.

Steven had Lotus 1-2-3 on his computer, but Jozef had no idea how to use it. He asked another employee to help him learn the application. After working until two and three in the morning for several days, Jozef grasped the concepts of creating formulas and using spreadsheets. He began loading all the plastics operational data onto the computer.

When Steven returned, he asked for his computer back. Jozef said no and then showed Steven all he had done. While Steven had modernized the business side of the company, Jozef was the first person at Arrow to use the computer to modernize the operations side. Steven decided to let Jozef keep the computer. He also decided that he very much liked how proactive Jozef was; soon thereafter, he took Jozef out of the management-training program and promoted him to production manager.

Chapter Nine

*I*n some ways, it almost seemed easier to purchase a million-dollar piece of equipment at Arrow than it was to get a decent calculator. When it came to spending money, production equipment was definitely the highest priority.

Mike Petrak, the man who helped Marcus's brother Manny escape communist Czechoslovakia, was brought to Arrow in the early 1960s to work as a purchasing manager. Mike eventually became responsible for both operations and purchasing and, in this role, determined which supplies were purchased and how they were distributed. In order to get a new pen, an employee would have to bring back the old, dried-out pen. A new pad of paper required the return of the cardboard backing of the old pad of paper. Another roll of toilet paper would be forthcoming only when the old toilet paper core showed up. When the women in accounts payable reported a large rip in the carpet, rather than replacing the worn floor covering, someone was sent over to sew up the tear.

In 1980, Roberta Frohardt started her career at Arrow as an accounting clerk. Working her way up, she eventually became an accounts payable manager. When she was still fairly new to Arrow, Marcus called her down to his office and began talking to her, asking her what she wanted to do professionally, how old her children were, and what her goals were in life. This was her first encounter with Marcus, and afterward, she wondered why some people felt intimidated by him. In fact, her manager had just told her, "If Mr. Rosenberg ever calls, you find me right away. I don't care where I am. Because when that man calls, we answer him."

Roberta didn't see anything in Marcus that day that even hinted at his being formidable. Rather, she found him to be a genuinely caring person. Because Marcus was so hands-on with what the company's expenses were, Roberta ended up working closely with him in her job as a payables manager. Her initial impressions of him grew into genuine respect because of his work ethic and the responsible manner in which he conducted his business.

One evening when Roberta was working late, Marcus came to her office upstairs and asked why she had not gone home yet. When she responded that she had a lot to do, Marcus began walking around the area. Noticing the many boxes of papers lined up along the wall, he questioned why they were there. Roberta explained that she had tried to get some file cabinets for the office, but her request had been denied by purchasing. Marcus sat down in front of Roberta's desk and asked her what supplies she needed. Roberta told Marcus which items would help her job, as well as the jobs of the other women in the department, become more organized and efficient. Marcus listened intently and, when she was finished, told her that he wanted to have a requisition on his desk the next morning for the file cabinets and other supplies.

Roberta filled out the paperwork and took it to the purchasing department. When she was told Mr. Rosenberg would never approve of the requested items, Roberta said, "If you'll just sign the requisition, I'll personally walk it over to him."

When she got to Marcus's office, he asked, "Are the file cabinets coming in today?"

"No, I wouldn't think so, Marcus," Roberta said.

"Okay," Marcus said, "then I want you to go back to the purchasing department right now and tell them that these cabinets are to be delivered today. Let me know when they get here."

The clerks in the purchasing department were stunned when Roberta returned with Marcus's orders, but they followed through, and shortly thereafter, the new filing cabinets were sitting in Roberta's office.

After she informed Marcus of their arrival, he showed up with two of his daughters, Helen and Margot. Marcus took off his jacket and rolled up his shirt sleeves. Then they all began taking the papers out of the boxes and filing them into the cabinets. Box by box was emptied until eventually everything was organized, cleaned up, and neatly put away.

Another time, Marcus called Roberta into his office, saying he wanted to ask her about something.

Without greeting or acknowledging her, Marcus said, "I want to know why some people don't tell me the truth."

Caught off guard, Roberta thought for a moment. Not sure exactly how to respond, she said, "Well, I think some people might be intimidated by you."

"Why is that?"

"Well, I don't know, Marcus."

At times, Roberta could understand how people might be unnerved by Marcus. From her vantage, it wasn't out of fear; it had more to do with Marcus's presence and his expectations. His presence was powerful and commanded respect. Marcus was demanding when it came to job performance and transparency of information. If employees couldn't give him the information he was seeking, he pressed harder for the answers until he got them.

In addition, Marcus was known to ask questions to which he already knew the answers. In this way, he could at times learn who was trustworthy and who might not be. Some people caught on to this tactic; others did not. Roberta thought that perhaps certain individuals told Marcus what they believed he wanted to hear so they would look more competent. Then again, maybe some people weren't fully transparent, because they were afraid of Marcus's reaction if they told him they didn't know the answers.

Although Roberta saw firsthand countless occasions when Marcus demonstrated kindness and care toward many of his employees, she had also heard that it was wise to avoid getting into a situation where he became angry with you.

~~*~*~*~*~*~*~*

Bill DeArmond worked with the Alexander Grant & Co. accounting firm while Arrow was in the process of going public. Bill had been out at Arrow's plant a few times, involved in some of the audits and other due diligence work. Another Alexander Grant employee went to work for Arrow, and sometime later called Bill to see if he'd like a job there as well. Bill was tired of the travel required at Alexander Grant and decided to join Arrow as a staff accountant in 1973. After six years of accounting, Bill moved over to inventory control cost accounting in the plastic extrusion department.

One of his new responsibilities was to go down to the production lines, see how the equipment was doing, and then report to Marcus any problems that might develop with the machines.

One day, Marcus called Bill to his office and said, "They keep shutting down one of the lines. Why are they doing that?"

"I don't know, Marcus. Let me go check."

Bill went downstairs to the maintenance manager and asked, "Why do you keep shutting down the line?"

"Because the SCR keeps blowing," the maintenance manager said. "They're two hundred ten dollars apiece. That's why I'm shutting down the line."

Bill returned to Marcus and told him, "They're shutting down the line because the SCR part keeps blowing, and they're two hundred ten dollars each."

"Well, why does the SCR part keep blowing?"

"That's a good question, Marcus," Bill said. "I don't know. Let me go back and ask."

At that moment, Marcus took off his glasses and threw them on the desk. Standing up, he extended his hands and banged the back of one hand onto the palm of the other several times, scolding Bill, "This is the way you learn the business! This is the way you learn the business!"

Bill learned from that point on to ask the right questions until he was fully prepared to report on anything to Marcus.

* ~ * ~ * ~ * ~ * ~ * ~ * ~ * ~ *

As director of food operations in the mid-1970s, Robert Gibson was responsible for all areas, including the bean room. Before the days of computerized inventory control, all stock was handled and tracked by hand. Some inaccuracies in the bean inventory were discovered when the shipping department could not find the needed product to deliver. Marcus went down to the warehouse to see what was going on.

"Robert! Get over here now," Marcus ordered.

Startled by Marcus's unusual demeanor, Robert said, "Yes, Marcus, right away. Is everything okay?"

"Robert, what is going on? The shipping department needs to send out some beans, but they can't find the product. Our inventory numbers say we have it in stock, but it can't be located. How can that be? Either your controls are totally out of whack, or you're stealing from the company!"

Unnerved by Marcus's accusations, Robert tried to defend himself: "No, Marcus! How can you say that? I've been here for years and have always been a loyal employee. You know I'd never do anything that would harm the company."

But Marcus continued on, demanding that Robert go out and personally count every single case of product in the warehouse and completely redo the inventory. Robert became so upset that tears began streaming down his face. Not long afterward, he collected himself and did what Marcus had asked, and the mix-up with the beans was resolved.

Chapter Ten

"Zucker Man! Zucker Man! Please report to your office right away."

Dropping what he was doing, Mike Zucker immediately headed to the front offices.

Mike had been working at Arrow since 1974 when he was eighteen years old. His father was Rabbi Max Zucker, the rabbi at Congregation Tiferet Israel, the Rosenbergs' synagogue. In fact, Marcus had been part of the search committee at Tiferet Israel that had hired Rabbi Zucker. The Zucker family lived down the street from Marcus and his family, and they all knew each other well.

Mike graduated from high school a year early and was attending Southern Methodist University, pursuing a degree in meteorology. His mother, concerned that he would not have a summer job, encouraged Mike to approach David Rosenberg. But Mike was too embarrassed to do that, so his mother had asked David if there might be a place for Mike at Arrow. David had brought Mike in and assigned him to the bean room to work on packaging and quality assurance.

At the end of Mike's first summer at Arrow, Marcus approached him and asked if he would take on a new position at the company as production scheduler in the bean room. The work would be very analytical, something that appealed to Mike, but moving over to this job would require him to change his schedule and attend college classes at night. Still, he liked the responsibilities the work would entail and accepted Marcus's proposal. Mike became so successful in this area that other departments began asking him to do their scheduling as well. Mike complied, and in addition to scheduling production, he began managing truck delivery timetables, optimizing routes, and making sure the loads were full. His job required him to be all over the plant all the time, and he was frequently paged over the intercom.

But this day, Mike was being paged to his own office, not to the shipping docks or the warehouse. Mike wondered if the page might be from Marcus. Mike's wife was pregnant with their first child, and he had been telling Marcus he wasn't making enough money to support a growing family. Marcus had not been as responsive to Mike's situation as he had hoped. When he stepped into his office, he saw Marcus there, and then he saw a huge stack of files on his desk.

"What are those?"

"Those are cities," Marcus said. "You are going to sell trash bags to cities."

"What do you mean?" Mike asked. "How am I supposed to do that?"

"Call up the cities, Mike. They buy lots of trash bags."

"What's in it for me, Marcus?"

Marcus's neck reddened.

"If you sell ten million pounds, I'll give you a fifteen thousand–dollar bonus."

"What about my regular work here at the plant?"

"That's your problem. After all, here is an opportunity to grow in the company."

Marcus turned and left the room.

Mike took the stack of files home, trying to figure out how he was going to sell ten million pounds of trash bags. Spreading a big map of Texas out on the kitchen table, he and his wife began going through the list of cities, highlighting the ones that bid out for their bags. In two months, Arrow was on all of those cities' bid lists. Mike went to Lancaster, Texas, and sold his first order, for fifty thousand trash bags. He was very excited—that is, until he realized the order amounted to 1,400 pounds.

Well, he thought to himself, *only 9,998,600 more pounds to go.* Mike kept at it, and with Marcus's guidance, sold fifteen million pounds of trash bags that first year.

When Marcus went to give Mike his bonus, he said, "No more bonus, Mike. This is now part of your salary."

Mike looked at him and said, "Thank you, Marcus."

"Oh, and one more thing. I want you to stop everything else you're doing around the plant and sell trash bags all day long."

So that was what Mike began doing. As he sold to municipalities, the Army Air Force Exchange, the US General Services Administration, and even the United Parcel Service (UPS), the trash bag business began to expand.

Marcus was pleased with this new consistent business, because he was able to use up excess scrap plastic leftover from production, which lowered his overhead costs and spread out the fixed costs. Marcus's brother David, however was becoming concerned that the production lines were being tied up for municipal trash bags, an item that did not bring in as big a profit as other products.

* \~ *\~ *\~ *\~ *\~ *\~ *\~ *\~ *

In the early 1990s, a great flood occurred along the Mississippi and Missouri rivers over the course of seven months. The flood was devastating to people, property, and crops in the affected regions—about 320,000 square miles. Some areas were flooded for almost two hundred days. Arrow partnered with Ryder Truck Rental to begin a relief collection effort for flood victims. The items collected were to be delivered to the Salvation Army in Iowa for distribution to those hard hit by the floods along the Missouri River. These items included canned goods, bottled water, baby food, paper towels, toilet tissue, and disposable diapers.

Arrow's goal was to deliver a forty-eight–foot trailer truck filled with goods. Arrow employees volunteered to man the collection effort, sorting, boxing and labeling the goods, and two Arrow drivers volunteered their time to drive the goods north from Texas. In addition, Arrow donated a large amount of paper plates, trash bags, and aluminum foil.

Arrow flood relief collection center

The collections efforts were very fruitful, and two weeks later, three trucks left Carrollton and delivered to two locations in Iowa and one in Missouri—both areas where the flood damage affected Arrow employees and customers.

Part Four

❧

The School

Chapter One

❧

On a quiet Saturday afternoon in the fall of 1960, Ann and Marcus sat at the kitchen table drinking coffee.

"Marcus, the children are getting older. Helen's already three, and she'll need to start school in the next year or two. And you know, our children are going to need to be in a Jewish school."

"I know, Ann," Marcus said. "We've talked about this already. But there's no Jewish school here now. The Hillel Academy closed down a couple of years ago, and I don't think this city even wants a Jewish school. It certainly didn't support the one it had before."

"Well, there's got to be some way to make this happen, Marcus. Because our children will be in a Jewish school, one way or another."

Then Ann got up from the table to check on Helen and Steven, who were just waking up from their naps.

~~*~*~*~*~*~*

One of Rabbi Rafuel Lowy's sons, Marcus, moved to Los Angeles after the war. When Marcus's son Rudy had his Bar Mitzvah in 1961, Marcus and Ann travelled from Dallas to California to attend the *simcha*. Rudy skillfully led the services, chanted from the Torah, and delivered a meaningful *d'var Torah* to the congregation. Afterward, Marcus went to his cousin and congratulated him.

"*Mazel tov*, Marcus. Rudy did a very fine job. I am most impressed with his skills and how much he knows about Judaism. He's in a Jewish school, right?"

"Thank you, Marcus. It's wonderful to have you here with our family; it means so much to us. And yes, Rudy's been in a Jewish school since preschool. We've been very happy with the teachers there and with what he's been learning."

"You know my children are getting older now. We want them in a Jewish school too, but Dallas doesn't have one right now. A few years ago, they had a day school, but the community didn't support it. I'm trying to see if I can help open a new school, but there are definitely some challenges."

"Well, good luck with that, and please let me know if I can help out in any way."

"Thank you. I'm hopeful we can get a project started. I'm planning to meet with someone from Torah U'Mesorah soon, and we'll see where we go from that discussion."

Not long after Marcus's trip to the west coast, the national convention for the National Jewish Welfare Federations was being held on a Friday through Monday at the Hilton Hotel in Dallas. Several attendees of the convention paid a visit to Marcus on Sunday afternoon. With Marcus were his two brothers, David and Manny, as well as Ann and some friends (Sol Prengler, Harry Goldman, Bernie Gerson, and Sol Schwartz). Jacob Lowy of the Montreal Jewish Federation and Irving Stone, president of American Greeting Cards of Cleveland, Ohio, joined Dr. Joseph Kaminetsky that day to talk to Marcus.

Dr. Kaminetsky, director of the National Society for Hebrew Day Schools (Torah U'Mesorah), was on a mission. Travelling around the United States going from city to city wherever a Jewish community existed, he set out to persuade the people in those locales to set up a Jewish day school. Dr. Kaminetsky was remarkably successful. When he first started out, only a handful of day schools existed in the country. By the time he completed his career, hundreds had been established.

Marcus was an easy sell for Dr. Kaminetsky. He knew that Marcus was already convinced of the need to build a new day school in Dallas. He was seeking only some guidance on how to best go about achieving the goal. Very real concerns existed, especially in light of the failure of the Hillel Academy just a few years before.

"Dr. Kaminetsky," Marcus asked, "how do we get into a new project like this when the one right before didn't succeed? How do we start over when everyone still remembers what happened—teachers not being paid and so forth? How do we build a Jewish day school in a community that doesn't seem to want one?"

In the early 1950s, the Hillel Academy day school had been established in Dallas. The school had not been supported by the larger Jewish community in the city, and finally unable to pay its teachers, it had to shut its doors in 1958. At the time of closing, Hillel Academy had had seventy-five students enrolled through fifth grade.

"Marcus," Dr. Kaminetsky said, "please come up to New York, and we'll talk some more. I will help you get your school started."

So Marcus travelled to New York to visit Dr. Kaminetsky. At their meeting, the two discussed many of the factors that Marcus would need to consider in getting a school started. During the visit, Dr. Kaminetsky also gave Marcus the opportunity to meet three rabbinical candidates to consider hiring as the school's first principal.

The first two candidates did not seem to have the right credentials or background, but the last candidate impressed Marcus. This young man had not only attended the Ner Israel Rabbinical College, a prominent yeshiva near Baltimore, but he was also a graduate of Johns Hopkins University. He had been the director of a Young Israel camp in Cleveland and was engaged to marry a woman who was graduating from a teacher seminary. The rabbi was very likeable, and Marcus wanted to bring him down to Texas so others could have the opportunity to meet him.

When Marcus asked the young man, Rabbi Mendel Bernstein, what conditions he would need to accept the principal position in Dallas, he responded that both he and his wife would need jobs at the school. In addition to his duties as principal, he would teach Jewish studies to the first graders while his wife would be in charge of the kindergarten. Marcus agreed to the proposed arrangement, and the two set a date for Rabbi Bernstein to visit Dallas.

Marcus was pleased that a candidate of Rabbi Bernstein's caliber would potentially be taking on the job as principal. In the meantime, other issues required attention. First and foremost, a new school needed funding and a place to hold classes.

Located in the southern part of the city, congregation Agudas Achim had served the small Orthodox community of Dallas for many years. As time had gone by, the Jewish population of the city, which had been largely concentrated in South Dallas, had migrated north. As a result, several congregations—Temple Emanu-El (Reform), Shearith Israel (Conservative), and Tiferet Israel (Traditional/Orthodox)—were founded in or relocated to the newer parts of town. While Agudas Achim remained in South Dallas, these other synagogues took root and grew.

Eventually, Agudas Achim decided to follow the Jewish migration patterns and move farther north as well. The timing, however, was not optimal. By the time the Orthodox congregation settled into its new facility, a small home located at 5608 Northaven Road, it was too late. The synagogue tried to build a critical mass in membership, but it was not successful, and long-term prospects of sustaining the shul looked bleak.

Marcus's cousin, David Lenovitz, lived in Dallas and had been very involved both with Hillel Academy and Agudas Achim. He and Marcus spoke at length about the synagogue's unfortunate predicament. It was in the course of these discussions that Marcus developed the idea of dissolving the synagogue and using the funds for something else, something with an eye toward the future. Marcus wanted the money for a new school. Why keep the assets tied up in a dying shul? Wouldn't it be better to take those funds and build an institution for the next generation of Jews?

To David Lenovitz, who was still disappointed by the closing of the Hillel Academy, Marcus's suggestion made a lot of sense. Marcus then spoke to Sol Prengler, Manny, David, and others, receiving their buy-in as well. But before moving forward with this plan, Marcus had to overcome a certain amount of resistance from some individuals in the shul establishment who did not want to shut down the synagogue.

In the end, the differences were resolved, and Agudas Achim closed its doors. Its property and building were transferred to the founding of a new Jewish school, as were the synagogue's cemetery and a large amount of cash. As part of the arrangement, the new school agreed to hold an Orthodox minyan until another Orthodox synagogue could be established in the area. This condition was formalized in the school's founding constitution.

~~*~*~*~*~*~*~*

When Rabbi Bernstein landed in Dallas, he half-expected to see horses running around everywhere. What he found instead was a metropolitan city with beautiful landscaping and very friendly people. The individuals he met initially were not native Dallasites; rather they were European men with European accents, many of whom spoke to him in Yiddish—Sol Prengler, David Lenovitz, Marcus, David, Manny—and all of them were sincere in wanting a Jewish day school to succeed in the city. They were fully aware that something was sorely missing from the community: a strong institution providing a solid Jewish education to Jewish children. Rabbi Bernstein unmistakably felt the Jewish values and *yiddishkeit* of these men and decided he would be comfortable working with them. He headed back to New York, happy that the interview had gone well.

All those who met Rabbi Bernstein liked him very much. Marcus decided to take one more trip up to New York, this time with Ann. Together they met with Rabbi Bernstein and his bride-to-be, Malkie. Marcus and Ann were both looking for the same traits in a principal-and-wife team. The new couple needed to be individuals who could easily mingle with the local Dallas Jewish population. While ritually observant themselves, they could not be perceived as religiously overzealous or as people who would try to turn Dallas upside down. The principal and his wife should be friendly and engaging and able to successfully promote the school to what was then largely a very secular Jewish community.

Just two days before their wedding, Rabbi Bernstein and Malkie were offered and accepted the jobs. Living arrangements were made for the couple, and they moved to Dallas six months before the school was to open its doors. After he arrived, one of Rabbi Bernstein's primary responsibilities was to build enrollment and raise community awareness of the coming day school. He was charged with encouraging people to become involved and enroll their children.

Rabbi Mendel Bernstein
Courtesy of Akiba Academy of Dallas

Rabbi Bernstein began taking out ads and writing articles about Jewish education for the *Texas Jewish Post*, the local Dallas Jewish newspaper. In addition, he and Marcus personally visited the city's congregational rabbis to talk about the school.

After Rabbi Levi Olan of Temple Emanu-El, the Reform congregation, visited with Rabbi Bernstein and Marcus, he politely but coolly wished them well. Though Rabbi Olan was very learned in Judaism and had grown up in a traditional home, he was an outspoken proponent of integrating Jewish children into the larger society. "Ghettoizing" them in a Jewish school was completely antithetical to his worldview. In his opinion, Jewish children should be in either public school or independent private schools, not sequestered away from the world. Likewise, Rabbi Olan was not a proponent of B'nai B'rith Youth Organization, a social group for Jewish youth, nor did he advocate sending Jewish children to Jewish summer camps such as Camp Young Judea. The Boys Scouts and Girl Scouts were just fine, as was the St. Marks School of Texas, but any other similar organization or institution that was distinctively or exclusively Jewish was not.

When Marcus and Rabbi Bernstein went to talk to Rabbi Hillel Silverman at Congregation Shearith Israel, they were received much differently—this time with a great deal of warmth and acceptance. Rabbi Silverman said that, as soon as the school opened, he wanted Marcus to come to Shearith Israel on a Friday night, because the rabbi planned to devote a sermon to the day school.

On the evening that Marcus and Rabbi Bernstein went to services at Shearith Israel, Rabbi Silverman pointed to the bricks of the sanctuary walls and passionately appealed to his congregants, "I need you to know that if you want these bricks to survive, if you want them to stay here after all of us are long gone, then you'll support this new day school for the children's education and for their future."

Rabbi Bernstein also started speaking to individual families about the school. The task was daunting, but Rabbi Bernstein was not completely on his own in this mission. Determined that the new school would not be another Hillel Academy, Marcus personally involved himself in all these startup efforts to ensure their success. For half a year, Marcus joined Rabbi Bernstein in going around Dallas almost every evening from house to house, talking to people and encouraging them to enroll their children as students. Other ground-level supporters of the school, such as Bernard (Bernie) Gerson and Ronald (Ronnie) Gruen, would sometimes join in these house calls. But in the beginning, only a very small number of people wanted anything to do with the new day school.

People would open their doors and say, "Oh, Marcus, we don't have any money to give to your school."

And Marcus would always reply in the same way: "I don't want your money. I want your children. I want your children to have a Jewish education. They need to have a Jewish education so they will stay Jewish."

The work was never-ending.

~~*~*~*~*~*~*~*

Marcus had come out of Auschwitz struggling with serious questions about God. Though he was profoundly silent about that period of his life, the effects of the war greatly impacted his personal theology. And yet, Marcus didn't live his life trapped in doubt; nor did he occupy himself with theological questions. He still loved being Jewish, and when the opportunity presented itself, he became fully committed to doing what he could to give children a strong Jewish education and identity. The best way for Marcus to dull the hurt in his heart was to give back to others, and in large part, he would do this by obligating himself to the next generation.

Marcus never wanted Hitler to win. The future and the continuation of the Jewish people had to be preserved. Therefore, it was crucial that Jewish children understand Judaism and what it represents. Only then could they make educated choices in life. For Marcus, the actual religious practice did not necessarily have to be defined, but the children needed to possess the knowledge of what Judaism is and what it stands for.

Chapter Two

Marcus's first involvement in community service to the Dallas Jewish community was not with this new school but rather with his synagogue, Congregation Tiferet Israel. At the very beginning of the 1960s, a new rabbi, Rabbi Sidney Weinschneider, had come to the shul. As part of his hiring agreement, a building committee had been formed to oversee the addition of a *mikveh* as well as a new sanctuary, updated kitchens, and a bride's room. Ann had encouraged Marcus to join the building committee, and he had become closely involved in the work of the project. The beautiful *aron kodesh* had been built for the sanctuary by architect Raymond Lambert and paid for by Marcus.

At that time, Rabbi Weinschneider had also set up a new preschool at the synagogue. The children enrolled in that preschool would become some of the first students at the new day school being established in Dallas. Rabbi Weinschneider had named the synagogue's preschool after one of the most famous Talmudic rabbis in Jewish history, Rabbi Akiba. While the preschool operated for only a few years, its name would live on.

On February 1, 1962, Dallas' new day school was founded as a nonprofit educational institution, chartered by the state of Texas. The school's first name was the Preston Hollow Day School, reflecting the name of the neighborhood where the school was located. The next year, the school's name formally changed to Akiba Academy of Dallas.

Marcus wanted a school that would grow and be successful. His vision for Akiba Academy was that it would have excellent teachers and be academically rigorous, teach about Jewish heritage, and instill a pride in Judaism. He also envisioned the students eventually attending college or university and fully participating in American life while, at the same time, applying Jewish values to the way in which they lived. The school was to be open and welcoming to families of all observance levels. Rabbi Bernstein's efforts in establishing the school reflected Marcus's vision.

Akiba kindergarten class circa 1969
Courtesy of Akiba Academy of Dallas

Initially, Rabbi Bernstein had concerns about how to build a Jewish day school based on Torah, knowing that many of the parents were very secular and had little to no involvement in synagogue life. The desire was to make the new school attractive to a wide variety of people while remaining true to Judaism. Parents needed to feel comfortable with the environment as well as secure in the understanding that their children would not be indoctrinated.

Aware that the school was expected to have an excellent general studies program, Rabbi Bernstein consulted with some of the premiere private schools in Dallas at the time, including St. Marks and Hockaday. He was given copies of their curricula as well as state requirements, to make sure the program was up-to-date and competitive. The English, science, math, and history teachers needed to be experienced and accomplished. Many would come from other private schools, most with master's degrees. All would be very qualified. Rabbi Bernstein did not want parents feeling that their children's educations were compromised in any way.

The rabbi was also looking for a certain caliber of teacher for Jewish studies—devoted educators who worked well with children and who would deliver a genuine and comprehensive Judaic studies program. He worked with Torah U'Mesorah to find experienced educators, but at the time, finding seasoned professionals willing to leave the comfort and stability of the New York area to come down to Texas was a challenge. Initially, the Jewish studies teachers at Akiba did not have years of teaching experience, but what they lacked in that regard was compensated for by a genuine devotion to the students and the community.

Ann was so appreciative of the Jewish teaching staff who moved down to work in the school that she brought lovely gifts to them at holiday time.

Marcus left Rabbi Bernstein in charge of building the curriculum, hiring talented staff, and creating strong programming. Moving forward, Marcus's involvement with the school was accorded elsewhere, with his main interests and general concerns being the financial pieces—budgetary issues, fund-raising, and capital projects.

In September of 1962, Akiba Academy opened its doors with three teachers and twenty-three students. Marcus's daughter Helen was in the first class. Tuition was three hundred dollars per year, and the school started with a budget of twenty-eight thousand dollars. The former Agudas Achim synagogue building became a school. The building, which was actually a small house, was about twenty feet wide and fifty feet long, giving the new students and faculty approximately one thousand square feet in which to operate. The two bedrooms served as classrooms. The living room/dining area was the "synagog-a-torium," which functioned as an auditorium, cafeteria, and synagogue. The garage had been converted into an office, and the women of the parent teacher association (PTA) cooked lunch for the children in the kitchen. On sunny days, the children were treated to physical fitness activities outdoors.

Akiba students exercising outside with their teachers
Courtesy of Akiba Academy of Dallas

Those who brought their children to that little schoolhouse felt like pioneers, innately understanding that they were on the ground floor of a very special enterprise, something with the potential to become quite impactful.

~~*~*~*~*~*~*~*

When Rabbi Bernstein first came to Dallas, he met with the leadership of the Jewish Welfare Federation to introduce himself and hopefully achieve some level of support from the agency for the new school. In those days, the Federation was largely run by members of Temple Emanu-El, a Reform congregation. From 1911 until 1954, every president of the Federation came from Temple Emanu-El. After that, a few of the presidents came from Shearith Israel as well.

In the early 1960s, Temple Emanu-El's Rabbi Olan was very well-established in the Reform community and held a great deal of sway with the Federation as well as with the local newspapers. At the time, the Reform movement in Dallas was very opposed to the concept of Jewish day school, especially a day school like Akiba Academy, which operated under the umbrella of Orthodoxy. In general, there was no particular interest in helping the nascent school succeed.

In Akiba's third year, Rabbi Bernstein received a phone call from someone at Temple Emanu-El who was affiliated with the American Council of Judaism, a lay group headed nationally by a Reform rabbi, Rabbi Elmer Berger. This group stood firmly against traditional Jewish ritual, Zionism, and the exis-

Akiba students coming to school;
Mr. Turner was the bus driver
Courtesy of Akiba Academy of Dallas

tence of the state of Israel. The individual who called Rabbi Bernstein was offering a ten thousand–dollar gift to the school if a small cosmetic change could be made to the Akiba school bus. On one side of the bus, the school name was painted in English; on the other side, the school name was in Hebrew. The person calling that day represented others who were very uncomfortable with this identifiably Jewish school bus driving all around North Dallas. The financial gift would be forthcoming if Akiba would make the Hebrew letters disappear. Rabbi Bernstein declined the offer.

~~*~*~*~*~*~*~*~*

With the closing of the United Hebrew Schools (an afternoon Talmud Torah) in the early 1950s, the Federation had discontinued its support of Jewish education in Dallas. However, Marcus knew that Federations in other parts of the country were helping the Jewish educational institutions in their cities. Against a backdrop of organizational resistance in Dallas, Marcus decided to formally submit an application for a monetary allocation from the Federation. While not necessarily enthusiastic with the receipt of the application, the Federation nonetheless allowed Akiba to begin the qualifying process. Any new agency requesting such funding was required to have certain prerequisites in place. Namely, the agency must be classified as a nonprofit. In addition, a functioning board of directors needed to be in place, and the agency had to be up and running for at least four years. Marcus set out to ensure that all those factors were taken care of. He became the first president of the school and, in keeping with that responsibility, continued to advance Akiba's case to the Federation.

In the meantime, Marcus was also reaching out and becoming well-known in the Dallas Jewish community.

Ronnie Gruen, an English-born immigrant, who was initially contacted by Marcus for financial help at the school, had become a dedicated and outspoken advocate of Akiba. Though he was entrenched in the Dallas community and taught adult Jewish courses at the Jewish Community Center of Dallas, Ronnie was not fully integrated into the American social scene and always felt somewhat like an outsider. In that sense, he and Marcus identified very well with each other. But Ronnie also identified with Marcus's mission at the school, even though he was not Orthodox himself. While Ronnie and his wife Ethel may have heard comments from some people who felt Marcus was pushing too hard, the Gruens saw him as a person with vision, a man with a "fire in his belly." Ronnie believed that, if Marcus didn't press forward, his dream for a new school would not take root in Dallas. Marcus took the necessary risks and was a very persuasive salesman and, all along the way, galvanized Ronnie and many others like him.

Marcus continued to approach the Federation, asking for its support. Ronnie did as well. While the leaders of Federation had a great deal of respect for Marcus's business acumen as well as for his charitable contributions, they did not see him marching to the same drummer as the majority of the community. His school was not something the Federation necessarily wanted to deal with. Still, Marcus didn't give up, and others in the community—people like Jacob Feldman, Reuben Wolfson, Mike Goldfarb, Ted Shanbaum—joined Marcus's efforts and supported his application to the Federation.

When the time came that Akiba had met the required prerequisites, the Federation acknowledged that it would have to figure out what to do with the school and Marcus's request for an allocation. A new committee was appointed to review Akiba's application, and with Marcus's encouragement, do a comparative study with seven other cities to see how they dealt with their day schools. Committee membership was diverse and included people from the Reform, Conservative, and Orthodox movements. Marcus was on the committee, and the chairman was a well-respected man named Milton Tobian, a member of Temple Emanu-El. At the time, Tobian was very involved in general educational issues in Dallas and took a genuine interest in Akiba.

The first discovery made by the committee was that, in every single one of the cities they looked at, the Federation gave a financial allocation to the local day school(s). They found an increasing national trend of Federation support for Jewish day schools, almost all of which were Orthodox at that time. Tobian wrote to the Federations in Los Angeles, Cleveland, and other cities to find out how that support had been born and in what manner it had developed.

Tobian then invested time into looking at Akiba itself as an institution. Going from classroom to classroom, he thoroughly examined the curriculum, parsed the programming, and visited with the principal and teaching staff. He spent six months investigating the school before he prepared the final report that, in the end, made a strong recommendation to the Federation board to accept Akiba's application and provide monetary support to the fledgling school.

With that recommendation, the next step was for the Federation board to come together to vote on the issue. Federation meetings were held at a location on Browder Street around the corner from the Baker Hotel in downtown Dallas. On paper, the Federation board had thirty-two members, including the community rabbis who were honorary members. Never in the history of the Federation to that point were all thirty-two members in attendance at any particular meeting. But the day the vote for Akiba was on the table, not one member was absent. Every member wanted to be there; members were either passionately for Akiba or vehemently against the concept of Jewish day schools.

Before the meeting took place, Rabbi Olan and another board member took Marcus aside and asked him why he was trying to harm the community. Why was he doing something that would split the Jews in the city?

"Rabbi Olan," Marcus said, "I'd like to respectfully say that I don't understand why you consider this grant application for the Federation as something that will cause problems and divide the community. By giving a few dollars to this school, the worst thing it will mean is that we guarantee to deliver to you educated members for your congregation."

The president of the Federation opened the controversial meeting by calling Tobian to present his committee's findings.

Tobian began by saying, "With all due respect to you, Rabbi Olan, I want you to know, based on my survey, you have failed in Jewish education."

The discussion from that point on was very heated. When it was Rabbi Olan's turn to state his position, he passionately declared that the school would divide the community. He articulated the need to maintain separation of church and state, foretelling the suffering of the public school system because of an exodus of students to Akiba. He concluded by predicting that the Federation would lose money from donors who disagreed with the agency allocating funds to a day school. More people spoke at the meeting—some for the school, others against.

A motion was carried and in the official vote, twenty-one board members were in favor of allocating funds to Akiba, three voted against it, and fourteen abstained. In 1969, the Jewish Federation of Dallas awarded

Akiba Academy ten dollars per month per grade school student. The first allocation was $9,270, but the amount of money given was never the issue. Rather, the matter was based on principle and whether or not a day school should be allowed to become a beneficiary agency of the Federation.

Rabbi Olan's prophecies were basically unfulfilled. The community was not split, and the public school systems continued to operate without interruption. However, the Federation did lose money; but it also made money. While some people stopped supporting the Federation because of its inclusion of Akiba Academy, others began giving to the Federation for the same reason. In the end, it had no financial bearing, and everyone eventually became used to the idea of the Federation supporting day school education in Dallas. Without Marcus, this likely would not have been the case for a very long time.

Chapter Three

$\mathscr{A}$s the day school drama unfolded at the Federation, Akiba was moving right along. Rabbi Bernstein was received very well by the community, and the school's new parents appreciated his sincerity and genuine interest in providing a high-quality program for the children.

Rabbi Mendel Bernstein teaching class circa 1966
Courtesy of Akiba Academy of Dallas

The PTA was also instrumental in getting the school up and running in many ways. Flora Robin was the first PTA president, and she helped form a nucleus of mothers, such as Hanna Lambert, Shirley Rovinsky, Thelma Gerson, Lee Veeder, Irene Meyer, and Naomi Benjamin—all of whom became soldiers for Akiba. In the school, they cooked lunches for the children and endlessly fund-raised monies for a variety of needed items, large and small. These women became a force of their own, going out into the community and spreading the word about the new school, urging their neighbors to enroll their children. The PTA mothers worked on getting their husbands involved in the school as well. These were extraordinary, devoted women who cared deeply and gave entirely of themselves to make certain that Akiba Academy would succeed.

For a number of years, Rabbi Bernstein taught a series of adult Jewish education classes to a group of interested Akiba mothers. The classes were based on a Jewish studies curriculum created by Torah U'Mesorah and covered a variety of topics, including Jewish philosophy and thinking, holidays, and history. Once or twice each week, mostly in the afternoons while the children were still in school, Rabbi Bernstein helped these mothers gain a deeper understanding of Judaism, giving them the opportunity to learn and discuss material they had never been exposed to. When certain blocks of study were completed, certificates were issued from Torah U'Mesorah acknowledging the women's successes. Upon receiving the certificates, the women were proud and delighted by how their knowledge of Judaism was advancing. Many of the women said that this knowledge was transforming their lives.

What was initially a very hard sell began to turn around. Parents were happy with Akiba, and students felt at home there. They enjoyed being at school and learning in its nurturing environment. The students themselves became very effective salespeople for Akiba as well. Once, when a student walked by the school kitchen and glanced inside, he pointed to a woman by the sink and commented to his friend, "Look! Mr. Rosenberg is married to one of the cooks!"

Akiba PTA mothers cooking lunch
From left to right: Ann Rosenberg, Hanna Lambert, Shirley Wald
Courtesy of Akiba Academy of Dallas

Rabbi Bernstein and the music teacher, Phyllis Stern, with Akiba students
Courtesy of Akiba Academy of Dallas

The original enrollment of twenty-three children grew quickly. Marcus knew that the school could not operate in the Northaven facility for very long, so he and the board began a capital campaign to construct a new building. Bernie Gerson, a parent and board member, found a 3.5-acre lot on Churchill Way, a couple miles north of the school's current location. Marcus and his brother David, along with Stanley Joe Schepps, purchased the eighteen thousand–dollar piece of land for the school. Then the challenging work of fund-raising began.

The new building would cost approximately $180,000 and was being designed by Abe Hershman; Paul Lewis was the contractor. The building committee consisted of Marcus Rosenberg, Bernie Gerson, Mike Goldfarb, Ronnie Gruen, Paul Lewis, and Reuben Wolfson. After colors and carpeting were chosen and other details were ironed out, the construction began in 1967.

Akiba Academy groundbreaking ceremony, Churchill Way
Courtesy of Akiba Academy of Dallas

While this project was in progress, the original Agudas Achim building in South Dallas was being demolished, and its cornerstone was on its way to the junkyard. Ronnie went to rescue the stone because of Agudas

Achim's direct connection to the founding of Akiba. Ronnie had the cornerstone loaded onto a rented truck and drove it to the school. A small ceremony followed, along with a discussion about the importance of the Jewish people's continuity.

Akiba Academy groundbreaking ceremony, Churchill Way
Marcus Rosenberg (left shovel), Paul Lewis (right shovel)
Courtesy of Akiba Academy of Dallas

On March 3, 1968, the school's new building was dedicated. With kindergarten and first through fifth grades in place, Akiba had an enrollment of nearly 150 students. Marcus welcomed the many guests, which included Mayor Erik Jonsson, at the dedication ceremony with the following:

The magnificent educational building that we are dedicating represents a great deal more than merely the new Akiba Academy.

We have erected a spiritually inspiring and aesthetically beautiful school, which the founders of our school never could possibly have envisaged when they inaugurated the first class in September 1962. However, the same fervor and idealism and dedication that motivated them several years ago has also motivated us in the construction of this edifice. We hope and pray that we may be worthy to continue in our new building the traditions and aspirations that have guided us so far.

On behalf of our officers and directors, I convey to each and every one a sincere mazel tov for this truly inspiring accomplishment.

May God continue to bless us in our labors.

Akiba Academy on Churchill Way property
Courtesy of Akiba Academy of Dallas

When Akiba was ready to move into the new facility, no money was left in the building fund. This was not a big problem, since the building itself was complete. However, there was no grass outside, only dirt. Various ideas were discussed on how to put in the landscaping, but in the end, instead of paying someone else to do the work, the parents, PTA, and board members decided to take on the job themselves. Everyone purchased plots of sod for one and two dollars and then, outfitted with work gloves and gardening tools brought from home, they all planted the school's new lawn on a warm Sunday morning. With a tremendous sense of ownership, together they marched ahead to make Akiba the very best it could be.

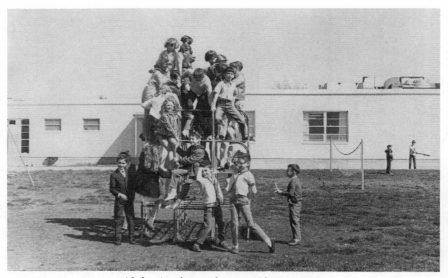

Akiba Academy playground circa 1970
Courtesy of Akiba Academy of Dallas

* ~ * ~ * ~ * ~ * ~ * ~ * ~ * ~ *

The original board of directors at the school was mainly composed of Akiba students' fathers—people such as Bernie Gerson, Paul Lewis, Mike Goldfarb, and Stanley Joe Schepps—most of whom were affiliated with congregation Shearith Israel. Some board members came from congregation Tiferet Israel, and a couple were from Temple Emanu-El.

One Sunday morning, Marcus and Ronnie Gruen set a time to meet with another Akiba father, Howard Schultz, for coffee. They had heard that Howard was the comptroller of the Sanger Harris department store downtown and thought he could be helpful to Akiba. The school needed some direction with finances at the time, so Howard began working with the bookkeeper to make sure the records were accurate. Because of his tremendous grasp of numbers and financial matters, Howard quickly gained respect from Marcus, and after a year or so, he was invited to sit on the board.

Marcus reached out to many individuals, bringing them into the fold. People who probably never would have thought of becoming involved with an Orthodox Jewish day school came to fundamentally identify with Marcus's mission and supported it wholeheartedly. Everyone involved felt a personal responsibility to make sure the school succeeded. Marcus instilled that spirit throughout the school.

Marcus's attitude toward running the school was that Jewish schools wouldn't show a profit; they always operated at a deficit. It was a foregone conclusion that enough money was never going to be available, so the school always had to go out and raise more. Dealing with budgetary issues in those days followed that same line of thinking.

At some point early on, it was determined that the school needed a bus, but nothing was in the budget for this item. Consequently, each board member threw in a few hundred dollars, and after that, of course, the bus could be purchased. Similarly, when more money was needed to help families with tuition, calls were made to either Marcus or Bernie Gerson, and the funds soon arrived at the school.

Marcus was also known to start an occasional board meeting with, "Okay, guys, we're going to be short next month, and we don't have enough money for the salaries." With that, all the board members would reach into their pockets and peel off bills until sufficient dollars were on the table. The board prided itself on never missing a payroll payment. At no time did the board members leave a meeting without having the funds the school needed. The individuals in that room were of one mind and one cause. Come hell or high water, the bills were going to get paid, and the school was going to be there the next day.

After going on like that for a number of years, the board members looked at each other and said, "My goodness, is this how we're always going to do things?"

The Akiba board had been like a "Good Ole Boys Network," with strongmen like Marcus Rosenberg, Ronnie Gruen, Howard Schultz, and Erv Rovinsky at the helm. And the PTA was getting frustrated. The women worked very hard and spent countless hours fund-raising for the school, and yet the PTA had no representation. Eventually a change came to the bylaws whereby the PTA president became a full member of the board of directors.

Akiba Academy's board of directors circa early 1970s

Front row, from left to right: Harry Goldman, Bernie Gerson, Walter Sussman, Sol Prengler, Ronnie Gruen, Marcus Rosenberg, Robert Kay
Back row, from left to right: Fred Time, Jerry Benjamin, Mort Robin, Manny Rohan, Henry Cohn, Dr. Joe Dubin, Sy Alhadef, Hartley Polasky, Paul Lewis, Charles Weiss, Leo Laufer, Leslie Schultz, Howard Schultz, Harold Rubin, Erv Rovinsky
Courtesy of Akiba Academy of Dallas

The first woman to sit on the Akiba board was Leslie Schultz, who was introduced by Marcus at her first board meeting with, "Gentlemen, we now have a lady in our midst. We're going to have to watch our language."

Ethel Gruen was the second woman on the board coming in as an officer, assistant treasurer. Before that, she was the first bookkeeper for the school. In the mid-1980s, Carole Ann Hoppenstein was the first female president of the school. She had served on many committees, including the education committee, which was very hands-on at the time.

Aside from the principal, almost every other function at the school ran on a volunteer basis. The education committee was involved directly with curricula and textbook selection and was very influential in determining the direction of the academic program. Many volunteers in those days spent as much time working for the school as they would have at a full-time job with pay, and they did this because of common values and shared goals. Akiba Academy and the children were at the very center of the volunteers' lives.

Akiba children saying good-bye at the end of a school day
From left to right: Mitchell Shrem, Jay Freireich, Alan Putter
Courtesy of Akiba Academy of Dallas

Akiba students enjoying lunch at school
Courtesy of Akiba Academy of Dallas

⁓⁓*⁓*⁓*⁓*⁓*⁓*⁓*⁓*

Marcus was president for the first eight years of the school's life. After that, the presidency was handed off to Marcus's close friend, Ronnie Gruen. As time went by, the board became more official, formalizing processes for bylaws, minutes, and other board business. Even after Marcus stepped away from the top position at the school, he was still very hands-on, especially with financial matters.

"Take ten percent off of the budget," he'd say every time a new budget was presented. Marcus always looked for ways to trim costs. He ran a tight ship and expected others to do so as well. Every cent was precious to Marcus, because his aim was for the school to be sustainable for the long-term. He never wanted to see a repeat performance of what had happened with Hillel Academy, a school that couldn't pay its teachers and had to close its doors. For Marcus, every cent meant Judaism and Torah and Jewish living for the next generation of children. Akiba was Marcus's pride and joy, and he felt a tremendous responsibility for its success.

Rabbi Bernstein leading a school assembly circa 1969
Courtesy of Akiba Academy of Dallas

⌐⌐*⌐*⌐*⌐*⌐*⌐*⌐*

The classrooms in the new building filled up, one by one. Before anyone else, Marcus saw the need to add a parking lot at the front of the property. Initially, only a long circular driveway was available at the school. Marcus pressed the issue and through a combination of fund-raising and Marcus's own fair share of funds for the project, the parking lot was built.

Marcus also saw the need to add a gymnasium to the building. Even though everyone said money was not forthcoming to put into such a project, Marcus insisted, pointing out that the school required a gym to retain families and continue drawing in new students. People didn't necessarily agree with Marcus, but because he was so insistent, they went along with it.

New students continued to enroll in the school, and the facility continued to expand to keep up with the growth—a new library, a new science lab, a chapel, a computer room. At some point in the early 1990s, however, they could no longer increase the size of the building on the ground; they had to look at constructing a second level. Akiba parent, Raymond Lambert, who had previously added the gymnasium, as well as the new chapel and science room, was set to be the architect and contractor for the proposed second-story addition. Shirley Rovinsky and Marcus's son, Steven, who was then the board president, handled the fund-raising for the new addition. Funding went well, but a question arose about the timing of the project. While Raymond thought that the work could be done in three months over the summer, Marcus did not agree with the assessment and advised against the timeline. In the end, the board decided to proceed with the project according to Raymond's proposal, and the second level was completed the day before classes started for the new school year.

By this time, Akiba had come to a point where no one person ran the business of the school; the board collectively took on that responsibility. Still, everyone knew that, without Marcus, Akiba Academy would have not been brought into existence. Every person involved understood that Akiba had been born and thrived because of Marcus's vision, passion, and dedication. He was the one who had inspired others to appreciate the mission of the school and take ownership of the institution.

Determined not to repeat the mistakes of Hillel Academy, Marcus worked tirelessly for Akiba to ensure that it would take root, succeed, and be sustainable for future generations. Akiba's success was never about

Marcus, nor was it for his own personal benefit or accolades. Every ounce of effort he put into the school was for the benefit of the children.

Akiba forever changed the face of Jewish Dallas. In very profound ways, the little day school that started out in a house was the catalyst for the other day schools and Orthodox institutions that would follow. Akiba Academy was Marcus's single greatest legacy to the Jewish community of Dallas.

Part Five

❧

The Shul

Chapter One

On Saturday mornings, Rabbi Bernstein davened at Akiba, where he served as the acting (unpaid) rabbi, and Sol Prengler filled the role of *gabbai*. Sol was responsible for almost everything, from ensuring a minyan for the service to preparing the food and spirits for kiddush. Akiba did not hold Friday night services, because the men did not want to compete with the services at Tiferet Israel. However, Saturday morning davening continued for many years, first at the school's original location on Northaven and then on Churchill Way.

The minyan was open, and those who participated were not required to pay dues. Because so many old-timers went to this service, it took on the nickname "The Elders of Zion." On Shabbat, the men would pull out tables and chairs, eat herring, have a *l'chaim*, and sing songs, swaying back and forth with their arms draped around each other's back.

After seven years of leading the school, Rabbi Bernstein left Dallas to return to his family on the east coast. The ad hoc Akiba minyan continued, mainly serving the school's successive teaching and administrative rabbis, as well as a small group of observant people living in the neighborhood.

⌐⌐*⌐*⌐*⌐*⌐*⌐*⌐*

In the mid-1970s, the Rosenberg Brothers Foundation purchased a half-acre piece of land for thirty-five thousand dollars on Churchill Way, down the street from Akiba Academy. Around the same time, Marcus had architectural plans drawn up for a synagogue that was designed with the Churchill Way lot in mind.

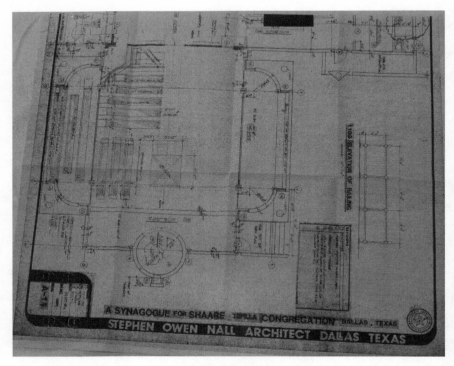

Architectural plans for Congregation Shaare Tefilla
Courtesy of Arthur David Zoller and Benjamin L. Zoller

However, nothing came of those plans until 1984, when Marcus called a meeting with his son Steven, Jeff Fine (Akiba parent and attorney), David Wohlstadter (Akiba parent and real estate developer), Moshe Levi (Akiba parent and physician), and David Greenblatt (Akiba parent and businessman). Marcus told them he was ready to move forward and build the shul he had dreamed of for years. Another Orthodox shul, Young Israel, had been established in the area a few years before and had a growing membership. However, Marcus envisioned a different type of Orthodox congregation, though he wondered how to go about creating such a synagogue without any congregants.

After discussing the situation for a while, the group came up with the "Field of Dreams" model.

"Look, you've got the lot. You've got the plans. And you've got the wherewithal to build," they told Marcus. "You can do this, even if you don't have any congregants yet."

Jeff and Moshe felt confident that, if Marcus would construct a building, there would be an instant congregation. Marcus went home and thought about all they'd said and subsequently decided that the approach was good.

Not long after, the men talked about the half-acre lot that had been purchased for the synagogue. They told Marcus the location was good but the size was far too small for the purpose of building a shul, and unless the acreage could somehow be expanded, the plan wasn't going to work.

As these shul planning meetings were getting underway, a developer was buying all the houses in the residential area where Marcus's lot was located. A new one hundred million–dollar, sixty-one–acre development—a gated-community called the Downs—was in the making. It was at that time that the developer made a call to Marcus. He needed Marcus's lot; it was located right where the front gate of the development was to be built.

This prompted another discussion between Marcus and his young confidants, which led to the conclusion that the lot could not be sold until an alternate site was secured. Nonetheless, an offer of $250,000 was made for the property, and Marcus told Jeff to tell the developer no. Then the price was raised to $400,000, to which the response was still no. An offer of $600,000 came in, and the answer remained "No deal."

At that point, Jeff said to Marcus, "You know, six hundred thousand dollars is a lot of money."

"Wait, Jeff, I'm going to do something," Marcus said. "Stay by the phone; you're going to get a phone call from the developer."

Marcus went out and found a bulldozer and had it taken over to the empty lot. One of his workmen began pushing dirt from one end of the property to the other. To a casual observer, it looked like the land was being leveled to begin construction work.

Soon enough, Jeff received a call from the developer who was very confused.

"What are you guys doing? I thought we were trying to work out a deal. What is it that you want?"

"It's not a question of the money," Jeff said. "We've been trying to tell you we need a large enough lot to build the synagogue."

The developer paused and then said, "But does it have to be right there at the entry of my development?"

"No, it doesn't," Jeff said. "It doesn't have to be in your development at all. As we've been saying, we just need a large enough lot in this general area. That's why we haven't been able to accept your offers."

"Okay. Okay," the developer said. "Don't do anything. Don't build anything. I'll get back to you."

As promised, the developer called back and told Jeff that he just bought four lots down at the other end of Churchill Way, to the west of Akiba Academy. The developer also threw in some seed money for the synagogue; in the end, Marcus was presented with four properties valued at more than one million dollars, plus the cash, all in exchange for the small lot he had originally purchased.

The deal was sealed.

The four lots were divided two by two, with an alley running between them. They were not platted together, and Jeff spent the next year or so getting them mapped as one lot and arranging for the city to abandon the alleyway.

David Wohlstadter began developing the plans. After delving in, he found that the design really wasn't optimal for a new synagogue. David and Steven told Marcus that they felt the shul wouldn't be large enough. In addition, no consideration had been given to making the building expandable, particularly the sanctuary. However, given the landscape of Orthodox Dallas at that time, Marcus did not agree with the points being made. He simply could not foresee anything to warrant a bigger synagogue than the one he had designed, so construction of the shul moved forward as originally drafted.

One day, Marcus called for Jeff to come to Arrow for a meeting with him. Jeff was a partner in a very large, very busy law firm, but if Marcus was calling, Jeff was going to go see him.

When Jeff arrived, Marcus said, "Jeff, I'm going to entrust you now with some promissory notes."

"What promissory notes?"

"They're for the shul ... the building of the shul, and you're going to hold them for me."

Jeff looked on Marcus's desk and saw the notes in fifty thousand–dollar increments, signed and dated—legally binding instruments. In total, eight hundred thousand dollars' worth of promissory notes—enough to cover the costs of building the synagogue—were stacked neatly in front of him.

"Marcus, what are they for?"

"For when it's time to pay the contractor. You'll come to me to redeem them."

Jeff didn't understand the reason behind issuing the notes. The land was owned by the Rosenberg brothers, and everyone knew the construction would be paid for by them as well.

"I still don't understand the point of having these, Marcus."

"I want people to know that I'm committed to doing this," Marcus said.

So Jeff took the notes, and whenever it was time to pay for any of the construction work, he would take a note over for Marcus to redeem it.

Another time, Marcus called Jeff and said, "Jeff, I need you to do something."

"What's that, Mr. Rosenberg?"

"I need you to go to the title company next Tuesday."

"What title company, Mr. Rosenberg? What for?"

"Jeff, you need to go to the title company. Sol bought a house."

"Mr. Rosenberg, please start from the beginning. Sol bought a house. What are you talking about?"

"Jeff, Sol bought the house next door to the shul," Marcus said. "You need to go to the title company and take care of it. Can you do that?"

"Yes, Mr. Rosenberg, of course."

Marcus said, "Good," and hung up the phone.

For some reason, the shul thought that the home next to the synagogue belonged to the school next door, the Dallas International School. But it did not, so Sol Prengler went over to the house and knocked on the door. When an elderly, sickly woman answered, Sol introduced himself as representing the synagogue and offered her $125,000 cash for the home. She accepted. Sol ran home, pulled a real estate contract out of his desk drawer, filled it in by hand, and gave it to the woman. He then called Marcus to tell him what was going on.

"Okay Sol," Marcus said, "that sounds like a good idea."

Hence, the perplexing phone call Jeff had received from Marcus.

When Jeff followed up with a call to Sol, Sol said, "Jeff, so nice that you called. You have to go to the title company next Tuesday."

"Which title company?" Jeff asked.

"You know," Sol said, "the one we use when we buy houses."

"And which title company would that be?" Jeff asked.

The conversation meandered along in this manner until Jeff received all the answers he needed. When Jeff showed up at the title company that Tuesday, sure enough, the deal closed without a hitch.

Chapter Two

❧

Once the decision was made to build the synagogue, a search committee was created to find a rabbi to lead the congregation. The search committee consisted of Marcus, his brothers David and Manny, Rabbi David Leibtag (the principal of Akiba), Rabbi Dov Dubovick (the director of Judaic studies at the school), Steven Rosenberg, David Wohlstadter, Jeff Fine, Bernie Gerson, Moshe Levi, David Lenovitz, and Cantor Max Wider. Yeshiva University in New York was contacted to put the word out that a new synagogue was forming in Dallas and looking to fill the rabbinic position.

In July 1986, Rabbi Howard Wolk, who had been leading a congregation in Patchogue, Long Island for nine years, came to Dallas to interview for the job. He stayed with Steven Rosenberg and his wife that weekend, and discovered that a typical one hundred–degree summer day in Dallas was not especially conducive to him wearing his trademark three-piece suits. Shabbat davening took place at Akiba Academy because only the shell of the new synagogue was in place. Rabbi Wolk delivered a sermon at services on Shabbat, and on Sunday morning after the formal interview, Marcus sat down with the rabbinic candidate to go over the drawings of the building and explain his vision for the shul.

Rabbi Wolk learned that Marcus was looking for this new synagogue to take its place among the other prominent synagogues in the city. Marcus did not want people viewing Orthodoxy as a second- or third-rate operation. By having an aesthetically pleasing building, Marcus also hoped to create a greater sense of permanence in Dallas, attracting professionals locally and from around the country. Much in the spirit of how Akiba had been established, Marcus also wanted the shul to be open and welcoming, not insular in any way. If someone were to drive to synagogue on Shabbat, that person should not feel judged. The synagogue would be Orthodox but, at the same time, engaged with the world. Such a synagogue would reach out to and partner with the broader Jewish community in Dallas. Marcus didn't want this synagogue to be "just" an Orthodox shul; he wanted it to be a community Orthodox shul.

Exterior of Congregation Shaare Tefilla
Courtesy of Arthur David Zoller and Benjamin L. Zoller

Rabbi Wolk identified with Marcus's vision, and in fact, the prospect of starting up this congregation in an up-and-coming city like Dallas was very alluring to him. Being the first rabbi of a brand new shul, helping to build something alongside the visionaries of the community was a tremendous opportunity the rabbi wouldn't pass up ... if he was offered the job.

Other rabbinic candidates applied for the position, but in the end, Rabbi Wolk's personality and warmth stood out. The committee was looking for someone approachable and who had good interpersonal skills and could work with individuals and families. They saw Wolk as possessing these traits; he was the preferred choice. Rabbi Wolk accepted the offer, and during Chanukah in December 1986, he and his wife, Annette, and their five children moved down to Dallas.

Courtesy of Arthur David Zoller and Benjamin L. Zoller

⁓⁓*⁓*⁓*⁓*⁓*⁓*⁓*

In the meantime, construction continued on the new synagogue. David Wohlstadter was the building chairman, and he met with Marcus almost every day during the project. Steven Rosenberg was also intimately involved in the building process. Many bumps, the crisis du jour, arose along the way—for example, the hot and cold water lines were reversed and had to be redone. But the building committee kept the project on track, and the new synagogue was completed with Rabbi Wolk at the helm.

Congregation Shaare Tefilla was established by Marcus and David in memory of their parents and younger brother, Aaron, all of whom had perished in the Holocaust. The aron kodesh in the sanctuary was constructed in the likeness of the aron from the Bikur Cholim synagogue in Bardejov, Slovakia, adorned with two golden lions at the top.

| Aron at Congregation Bikur Cholim, Bardejov Courtesy of Meyer Denn | Aron at Congregation Shaare Tefilla Courtesy of Arthur David Zoller and Benjamin L. Zoller |

The beautiful structure designed to hold the *sefer Torah* in the Dallas synagogue was decorated with stained glass and bore the Hebrew words meaning, "I have set Hashem before me always" (Psalms 16:8), engraved across the front.

While its foundations were rooted in the honor and memories of the past, congregation Shaare Tefilla was built for a new community in the new world. During construction, the kitchen was intentionally left undone—with bare concrete and no electrical outlets—so that the congregants could finish it. The Rosenbergs paid for the shul, but Marcus wanted the community to take ownership of the new enterprise.

This new enterprise, this Orthodox synagogue, ended up being formed in a completely unorthodox manner. Nearly every other synagogue comes about when a group of like-minded people organically grow large enough to hire a rabbi. Then, when they reach a critical mass and attain the funding needed, a building is built. But not Shaare Tefilla. Through the generosity of Marcus and his brother, David, the land for the shul was acquired and the building was constructed and paid for. From there, a core group of ten families embarked on a search and brought in a new rabbi. Then the synagogue opened its doors. By the end of its first week, Shaare Tefilla had some fifty new member families.

Sanctuary at Congregation Shaare Tefilla
Courtesy of Arthur David Zoller and Benjamin L. Zoller

The beginning of Shaare Tefilla's life was a very exciting time. The synagogue hosted many events so the congregants could get to know each other and the new rabbinic couple. Initially, the Wolk family lived in the shul's small house, which was located behind the synagogue parking lot. On their first Shabbat, they went to the Akiba principal's home for lunch. When they returned to their house, the key didn't work, and the Wolks were locked outside for quite some time. It was fortunate that the family had felt so welcomed by the community; otherwise, they might have gotten the wrong message—that perhaps the key no longer fitting in the lock hinted at Rabbi Wolk having a very short career in Dallas!

Moshe Levi became the first president of the board, and he and Rabbi Wolk began mapping out a path for the shul. In addition to social events, the shul began to offer a large variety of classes in order to continue drawing new people into the synagogue. The membership numbers grew steadily, week after week, month after month, and the influx was thrilling to everyone involved.

Rabbi Wolk made a very focused effort from the beginning to become involved in communal activities. He felt the Orthodox community in Dallas could not and should not build walls around itself.

The Federation was one of the agencies Rabbi Wolk first approached, attending nearly every meeting. Usually, he was the only rabbi there. For many involved in the Federation, Wolk was the first Orthodox rabbi they had ever met. Rabbi Wolk was engaging and very likable; so much so that, in 1989, several weeks before a Federation mission was scheduled to leave for Israel, Steven Waldman, the lay leader of the mission, contacted Wolk to invite him to go on the trip. Several people had gotten together, some from Shaare Tefilla and some from the Federation, and purchased a ticket for the rabbi. Wolk accepted the invitation, and the experience was so positive for him, as well as for the mission participants, that he went on eight additional trips after that. From that point on, the Federation always invited a rabbi to accompany its missions to Israel.

Rabbi Wolk taught many classes both in the shul and in other venues, such as the Joys of Jewish Learning at the Jewish Community Center. And like Rabbi Bernstein, the first principal of Akiba, Wolk wrote articles and op-eds for the *Texas Jewish Post* and the local Dallas newspapers. He was the chairman of the Israel Commission for Jewish Community Relations Council; he served as the rabbinic chairman at the Va'ad Hakashrus of Dallas; and he sat on various committees at Jewish Family Services. Rabbi Wolk was also a very engaged activist for Soviet Jews, fighting for their rights to immigrate to Israel and other countries. Under Wolk's direction, in December of 1987, a delegation of some twenty-five Shaare Tefilla members attended a massive rally for Soviet Jewry in Washington DC. Theirs was the largest group participating from Dallas.

In addition, Wolk was the first Orthodox rabbi ever to join the

Rabbinic Association of Greater Dallas, a group representing all Jewish denominations in the city, including at times, female Reform rabbis. By bringing the topic of divorce to this council, Wolk also spearheaded a community-wide campaign publicizing the importance of divorcing couples to "Get a *Get*."

Rabbi Wolk's communal involvement in the larger Dallas Jewish scene was far-reaching, as was his work in the Orthodox community. Partnering with several lay leaders, Wolk helped to establish a formalized Chevra Kaddisha to meet the needs of not only Shaare Tefilla but the community as well. Marcus had seen the necessity of an *eruv* for quite some time, and Rabbi Wolk, along with Rabbi Nata Greenblatt from Memphis and Shelly Rosenberg, undertook establishing one in the late 1980s. Jeff Fine assisted their efforts by working with the city to attain all the needed permits, a time-consuming process. The eruv became operational in 1991. Rabbi Wolk taught in the day schools and was involved with conversions as well.

As a result of Rabbi Wolk's outreach and hard work, many processes in the Orthodox community were formalized, providing a richer and more authentic experience for Jews living in Dallas.

From left to right: Rabbi Howard Wolk, Marcus Rosenberg, Sol Prengler

185

During the early years of Shaare Tefilla's life, the shul ran very much like a business, with Marcus acting as the chief executive officer (CEO). Marcus would sometimes jokingly refer to himself as "The Godfather." Though he was never an officer or a member of the board, he clearly directed certain activities—not the day-to-day, but those specifically dealing with finances.

Sometimes the board president, along with another officer, would meet Marcus at his home, sit in his office, and discuss the various financial needs of the shul. Marcus might ask a question or two; then he would turn his chair to face the credenza behind his desk. On top of the credenza was an old-fashioned check-writing machine. Marcus would put in a blank check, fill in the amount—which might be anything from ten thousand to one hundred thousand dollars—and then slide the check across the desk. Nothing else. He'd just slide the check across the desk.

In those days, Marcus's and David's money bailed Shaare Tefilla out of many situations. The brothers basically funded the whole shul, not just the building but the operating budget as well. Because the synagogue was dedicated to the memory of their parents and younger brother, the success of the institution was of great importance to Marcus and David.

Dedication plaque at Congregation Shaare Tefilla
Courtesy of Arthur David Zoller and Benjamin L. Zoller

Marcus was involved in other ways at Shaare Tefilla as well. Singing Jewish songs and prayers had always been one of his loves in life. Marcus had led the davening for many years at Tiferet Israel on the high holidays, and despite the fact that years of smoking had negatively affected his voice, he still enjoyed chanting the high holiday prayers as well as the Shabbat davening in front of the congregation at Shaare Tefilla.

Marcus and his brothers observed *yahrtzeit* for their parents and youngest brother on Simchat Torah, since that was the time of year when their relatives had been shipped to Auschwitz to meet their fate. With aprons on, Marcus and Manny would stand in the shul kitchen before services, cutting up herring and slicing purple onions for the kiddush they were sponsoring. In addition, Manny would lead the holiday *mussaf* davening, always with tears in his eyes and a great heaviness in his expression, especially when he reached the blessing about a God who brings the dead to life.

The youth of the shul were also very important to Marcus, as were the youth of the school. He saw an opportunity at Shaare to engage the young people, reasoning that a shul in the twentieth century must have activities to keep the young people interested and eager to come to synagogue. Because of Mike Zucker's many years of youth programming experience at Tiferet Israel in earlier years, Mike was approached by Marcus to spearhead and lead this programming at Shaare Tefilla. In their conversation, Marcus said repeatedly, "Our future is our youth." Mike accepted Marcus's proposal and started a junior congregation for the first through seventh graders. He was involved in this area of service to the community for many years.

Part Six

The Man

Chapter One

When Marcus's young children woke up in the morning, their father was at work already. When they went to sleep at night, Marcus was still working, either at Arrow or in the community. But on Shabbat, Marcus was home with his family.

Friday nights were special, the highlight of the week when everything stopped and the family could sit down together for a meal. With the candles glowing from the dining room breakfront, the family welcomed the Sabbath with "Shalom Aleichem." Then, with his deep soulful voice, Marcus chanted the blessings over the wine and challah. Ann served a beautiful, delicious Shabbat meal.

The Rosenbergs entertained guests almost every Friday night. Marcus's young children would watch their father interact with their company, seamlessly weaving through conversations on history, religion, and Halacha, with words of Torah often interlaced into the topics at hand. Just from these short discussions, they saw the vast knowledge their father possessed on so many different subjects.

After the meal, the family and guests sang *zmirot*. Sometimes, the kids would sing some of the songs they had learned at school. In general, Marcus wasn't particularly demonstrative or physically affectionate with his children, but during *Shir Hamalot*, he let the children take turns sitting on his lap until the *Birkat Hamazon* began. Sheri and Lizzy would fight to get to their father first. They wished the song would go on forever.

The holidays were special times as well, especially Pesach. During the early years, the *seders* were very big, with a lot of relatives descending upon the Rosenberg residence. The Sigels would stay with them, and sometimes relatives from Austin and other cities would join in as well.

Front row, from left to right: Sheri Rosenberg, Rose Tanenbaum, Ann Rosenberg, Marcus Rosenberg, Lizzy Rosenberg
Back row, from left to right: Margot Rosenberg, Steven Rosenberg

Marcus always led the seders. He loved the *chazzanos*. Searching for the *afikomen* was a treat for the children. One year, when Erika's daughter, Karen, was about four years old, she found the afikomen. Marcus presented her with a five-dollar bill, and the rest of the children received two dollars each. Karen cried, though, because her siblings and cousins received two pieces of money, and she got only one. As the years went by, the afikomen winner would go with Marcus to the toy store to pick out his or her gift on a later day.

From left to right: Manny Rohan, Marcus Rosenberg, Erika Sigel, David Rosenberg

Sukkot was a treat for the Rosenbergs, especially Marcus, whose *sukkah* was the fanciest one in town. He put carpeting on the ground and spent hours each year decorating the walls and ceiling. When everything was done, he took great pride in the final result. The wooden structure would be filled with family and friends throughout the week, everyone enjoying each other's company, Ann's delicious fare, and Marcus's famous sukkah.

Marcus was a very skilled ping pong player, and he enjoyed bowling as well. Every so often, he took his children to the bowling alley on a Sunday. He would also take his daughters to Northpark Mall to go shopping for a new dress or outfit for Rosh Hashana or some other special occasion; Marcus liked his women dressed well. If Ann's birthday was coming up, he'd bring along a daughter or two to help him pick out her gift.

The family also took vacations, mostly domestically. On those trips, Marcus would spend much of the time on the phone, working. Arrow had a condominium in Acapulco, and every now and again, he went down there with one of his children for some one-on-one time. They relished those occasions with their father.

Marcus and Ann took numerous trips together over the years, many of them abroad. They travelled with Erika and Andy Sigel and sometimes with Marcus's cousin, Jack Nagel, and his wife Gita.

Marcus at a family dinner in the 1970s with his daughter, Helen

Chapter Two

In 1969, Marcus joined a search committee at Tiferet Israel. The shul was in need of a new chazzan and ready to bring in a candidate, a talented young man who was already serving in a congregation on the East Coast. Yitzchak (Yitz) Cohen was born in Krakow, Poland, in 1949 and raised in Jerusalem. While he was a young child, his natural vocal talents were discovered. He was called a *wunderkind* and received invitations to perform throughout Israel and Europe. At the age of seventeen, he was hired as cantor of Congregation Ohev Shalom in Washington, DC.

In February 1970, the young cantor was brought to Dallas to interview and perform at Tiferet Israel. When Marcus and Yitz were introduced to each other, they immediately clicked, brought together by their common Hasidic upbringing and, even more profoundly, by their love of the Yiddish language and passion for cantorial singing. The shared languages between Yitz and Marcus became Yiddish and music; the threads that bound their relationship were yiddishkeit and a deep devotion to Judaism.

When Yitz moved down to Dallas, Akiba Academy was graduating its first class. Yitz attended the school's commencement at the new building on Churchill Way. Marcus asked the new principal, Rabbi Shlomo Jakobovits, if Yitz could teach at the school. It was very important to Marcus that the children know how to daven the Shabbat prayers with the old *nusach*, the right style, the right melodies. For two years, Yitz imparted the old-world style of davening to the pre–Bar Mitzvah children of the day school.

When Marcus travelled, he sometimes saw recordings that he thought Yitz might enjoy and brought them back to his friend. Marcus even offered singing advice to the cantor, "You know, Yitz, if you do a little *dvrei* over here instead of over there, it would sound much better." Yitz always received Marcus's suggestions with a big smile.

Marcus led davening for the high holiday *shacharit* services at Tiferet Israel for many years, bringing with him the nusach he had learned as a boy in Bardejov. After Yitz joined the synagogue, Marcus went to him every year before the holidays and proudly shared some new melody he'd learned, excited to find a prayer to adapt to it. He would sing the melody to Yitz no matter where they were. Whether they were having a drink between shacharit and mussaf in the meat kitchen at shul or on their walk home from Shabbat services, Marcus would sing and Yitz would sing, the two of them together, each man filled with passion and joy.

~~*~*~*~*~*~*~*

To some people, Marcus came across as very reserved. But Marcus had a number of close, trusted friends. Sol Prengler, Ronnie Gruen, Yitz Cohen, and Reuben Wolfson were all part of his *chevra*. So was Sol Schwartz. Originally from Holland, Sol had met Marcus in Dallas when Dwight Eisenhower was still president. Sol's family was one that Marcus had recruited to attend Akiba during its early years. Sol was a founding member of Shaare Tefilla, and he always sat next to Marcus in services, because they liked to *schmooze* together. When Marcus received an honorary doctorate degree from Bar Ilan University, he asked Sol to join him at the ceremony in New York. Sol was a true friend to Marcus, never expecting anything other than companionship.

Marcus was also close with Rabbi Mendel Dubrawsky, the first Chabad rabbi in Dallas. Ronnie Gruen brought Chabad to the city in the mid-1980s, and Marcus quietly supported Dubrawsky's efforts, financially backing many of Chabad's programs in the community.

Every year when it came time for Yom Hashoah, Dubrawsky had an activity for singles in the city. Usually he'd bring in a Holocaust survivor to speak about the horrors of those years as well as his or her own personal tragedies. At a certain point, the group was looking for something different. One year in the early 1990s, Dubrawsky invited Marcus to speak at the event. Dubrawsky did not know what Marcus was going to say, nor did he prepare him beforehand. He only knew that Marcus had said he was not going to talk about all the bad things that had happened to him.

Marcus began speaking in front of the group on the topics of survival and the mind-set he had sustained during those years to make it from one day to the next. Marcus told the crowd that he had always tried to look past the moment, stay positive, and seek a solution for any obstacle that came his way. He had taken risks that others hadn't. In the darkest of times, he had never pitied himself; he did not paint himself as a victim. As long as he could breathe, as long as he could do, he had known he had choices. He always tried to have a plan, and that had given him the freedom and the strength to survive.

The audience clung to every word he said. Uplifted by his message, they did not want him to stop speaking that day.

Marcus at the groundbreaking of a Chabad facility
Marcus is holding the second shovel from the right

Though Jack Nagel was Marcus's cousin, he was also a close confidant, especially in the later years. The two had a shared history. Both had been sent to Auschwitz together; both had survived the horrors and losses of the war. The bread that Jack had shared with Marcus in the concentration camp had become a standing routine between the two. Jack would ask for half the money it had cost him to buy the bread, and Marcus would joke that he had half a loaf of bread in the kitchen for Jack to take home. But the two men had other commonalities as well.

First, both were very successful businessmen. And Jack's wife and Marcus's wife were very close. Most importantly, Jack and Marcus were strong believers in giving back and doing good in the world. While Marcus was involved in Jewish education in Dallas, Jack was involved in the same types of institutions in Los Angeles. Jack and Marcus each bought an apartment in the same building in New York City, and every time they were there together, they talked about their communal and charitable work.

One time, Jack told Marcus he had gotten involved with Bar Ilan University in Israel. Fifty acres sat empty on the Bar Ilan campus with no facility yet for Jewish education, so Jack had donated the money for a building. Since Marcus identified with the philosophy of the institution, Jack told him he should look into giving to Bar Ilan as well. Putting him in touch with the president of the university, Jack gently nudged Marcus toward the multimillion-dollar donation he would make for the university to build a new music building on campus at the beginning of the twenty-first century.

Chapter Three

❦

*M*arcus was on the board of the Orthodox Union (OU) for many years, and in the early 1970s, the OU honored him with the Kesser Shem Tov award. The award was presented in New York, but for those who couldn't travel to the formal dinner, the OU sent a representative down to Dallas. Dallas' mayor, Robert Folsom, was present for the small ceremony honoring Marcus. Several people from Dallas also flew to New York for the national ceremony. Accompanying Marcus was his brother Manny, as well as Rabbi Max Zucker and Cantor Yitzchak Cohen from Tiferet Israel. Noted author and Holocaust survivor Elie Weisel was the keynote speaker at the dinner.

In his speech, Weisel chastised the Orthodox rabbis of Europe for their role in the unfolding tragedy of the Holocaust. When the rabbis had told their communities not to fight and not to resist the Nazis because whatever happened was God's will, they helped to accelerate and multiply the losses many times over.

"See now what you did to our people," he cried out, refusing to allow anyone in the ballroom to rebut his statements.

Manny couldn't believe his ears. Weisel echoed his own sentiments exactly. The Jews should have fought back instead of passively marching into the gas chambers like sheep to the slaughter. Because of his personal losses in the war, Manny still struggled mightily with God and Judaism. Afterward, he approached Weisel to share his thoughts.

"How is it that you and I went through such similar experiences in

Europe, and yet you still maintain your faith and remain so strongly Jewish?" Manny asked.

"That prerogative God did not give to me—that Judaism should stop with me. I must carry on and perpetuate the Jewish people because we have a right to live," Weisel said.

~~*~*~*~*~*~*~*~*

Marcus gave generously to community organizations. He founded Akiba Academy and Shaare Tefilla and continued giving substantially to those institutions, as well as to Yavneh Academy, throughout his life. He also quietly gave to other organizations, such as the Vogel Alcove, a day care center for the children of homeless people trying to find work. He donated to the North Texas Food Bank and to the Jewish Home for the Aged. He was generous with the Jewish Federation of Greater Dallas, American Israel Public Affairs Committee (AIPAC), Israel Bonds, and Torah U'Mesorah.

From left to right: Israeli Prime Minister Yitzhak Rabin, Marcus Rosenberg, Ann Rosenberg, Howard Schultz, President Bill Clinton

For Ann and Marcus Rosenberg
With best wishes,

Al and Tipper Gore

From left to right: Al Gore, Ann Rosenberg, Tipper Gore, Marcus Rosenberg

Marcus and Ann set up a fund at the Dallas Jewish Community Foundation to provide scholarships to students from the southwest region of the United States who wanted to attend Yeshiva University. The Rosenbergs donated a museum room at the Center for Jewish History at Yeshiva University and paid $3.5 million to Bar Ilan University in Israel to construct a new music building.

Marcus was honored by several of these institutions, including Akiba Academy, Torah U'Mesorah, Bar Ilan, and Yeshiva Toras Chaim in Denver.

Sign at Bar Ilan University announcing the Rosenbergs' music building

In the late 1960s and early 1970s, a number of Jewish Federations around the country were establishing Foundations for the Jewish communities in their cities. Such foundational agencies are set up to professionally manage and administer funds donated by individuals and organizations for the benefit of charitable and philanthropic causes.

In 1973, Marcus was one of a handful of community leaders, including Ervin Donsky, Dr. Stanley Pearle, and Murray Munves, who helped establish the Dallas Jewish Community Foundation, originally instituted as the trust and endowment arm of the Jewish Federation of Greater Dallas and the organized Jewish community. Marcus remained very involved with the Foundation during its formative years.

In 1989, when Marcus was honored by Akiba Academy at its annual fund-raising dinner, he stepped up to the podium, pulled a folded sheet of paper from his coat pocket, opened it up, and began to speak. The paper he read from was more than twenty years old and contained the words he had spoken at the founding of Akiba.

When he finished, Marcus looked up and said, "I gave this speech over twenty years ago and spoke about how important it was to have a Jewish day school in Dallas. Tonight, I'm standing in front of you to tell you the same thing applies—only this time we need a high school. Too many people are leaving the community because we don't have one yet. I'm pledging a trust fund to support a high school, and we need to work together to get it done."

While the actual startup work and funding for a new Jewish high school in Dallas was taken on by others, Marcus planted the seed that night in front of the community. In 1992, Yavneh Academy of Dallas was established.

Ann and Marcus Rosenberg at the Akiba Academy dinner honoring Marcus in 1989

In the early 1990s, a new Holocaust museum was being planned in Washington, DC. Marcus had recently returned from a trip to Spain with the American Jewish Congress. While in Spain, Marcus had visited a shul in Toledo, where he had seen a small plaque on the wall saying that Jews had lived in the area in 1492. It was the land of the Golden Age, where a magnificent Jewish community had once flourished, and all that was left now was this small shul and a plaque. Marcus did not want the vast and once-vibrant Jewish communities of pre–World War II Europe and the subsequent horrors of the Holocaust to become just another footnote in history.

Though Marcus had not generally been interested in Holocaust memorials, he heard that some prime real estate in DC had been acquired for the new museum. Marcus called the museum planners and told them he would like to come up and see what they were doing. They asked his name and, when they didn't recognize it, told him they would call back. The museum planner called Marcus back fifteen minutes later after doing a little research and told him he would be very welcome to come up to DC anytime to visit. He flew up the next day to take a tour of the construction site. Marcus asked how much it would cost to become a founder. When they told him a million dollars, he quickly agreed.

Marcus Rosenberg in Washington DC at the time of the US Holocaust Memorial Museum dedication

The reasons Marcus decided to fund the DC museum were threefold. First, he was very impressed with the research they were conducting as well as the scientific and precise manner in which they were gathering documentation for the library. Second, the miniature model of Auschwitz that the museum had constructed made an impression on him; the layout was exactly as he remembered. Third, the location of the US Holocaust Memorial Museum was optimal in a high-traffic area of the nation's capital. Marcus invested in the institution because he knew a large number of people would visit and learn from the evidence presented at the museum that the most sophisticated and civilized country in Europe had developed the most efficient and effective ways to murder men, women, and children in order to annihilate a people.

* ⁓ * ⁓ * ⁓ * ⁓ * ⁓ * ⁓ * ⁓ * ⁓ *

Marcus gained a reputation of giving generously to charities large and small. At Arrow, a steady stream of black hat rabbinic visitors, mostly from the New York area, could be seen in the front office, looking for *tzedakah*. As long as their organizations were officially classified as nonprofits, Marcus always gave to them.

Marcus's public acts of charity, particularly for Akiba Academy and Shaare Tefilla, were well-known, but he was also involved in countless acts of private charity and assistance to which most people were not privy.

Around 1980, Yitz Cohen headed to Israel to celebrate Pesach. Before Yitz left, Marcus went to Yitz with ten thousand dollars and asked him to distribute the money to needy families. Though Yitz told Marcus he was uncomfortable travelling with so much money, Marcus insisted. Yitz gave the money to a dear friend, Rabbi Raphael Binyamin Levine (son of Rabbi Aryeh Levine), who in turn disbursed the funds to a number of families in Jerusalem. Yitz took many trips to Israel, and Marcus often gave him tzedakah to pass on to those less fortunate in Eretz Yisrael.

Marcus helped Yitz out personally on several occasions as well, including the time Yitz was very ill in 1997. By then, Yitz was the rabbi of Tiferet Israel. He was in a coma in the hospital, and Marcus had heard from a mutual friend, Duke Rudman, that Yitz might not have sufficient health coverage. Marcus and Duke rushed down to the hospital to talk with Yitz's wife, telling her that they would take care of any medical expenses the insurance wouldn't cover.

Back row, from left to right: Ann Rosenberg, Rabbi Yitzchak Cohen, Rosie Cohen
Seated: Marcus Rosenberg

After spending seven years at Akiba Academy, Rabbi Mendel Bernstein left Dallas to go back to the East Coast and into the family wholesale grocery business. Fourteen years later, he attained his broker's license and went to work for Merrill Lynch. During all those years, he and Marcus stayed in touch and maintained a close friendship. Marcus was always concerned for Bernstein and his professional success. Once Bernstein became a broker, Marcus invested huge sums of money with the brokerage house, becoming his friend's absolute biggest client at Merrill Lynch and raising his stature in the firm.

When a business acquaintance of Marcus's lost his brother-in-law in a plane crash, he came to Marcus for support. To help his sister, the man was trying to sell off his brother-in-law's office supply business. Though Marcus expected his wife Ann to spend judiciously and his company was very frugal when it came to office expenses, he nonetheless had a soft spot in his heart for those in need. After this man asked Marcus if he would purchase some of the leftover inventory, Marcus bought a fifty-year supply of paper clips at prices that were higher than he would have paid at the retail office supply store around the corner. This was certainly not within Marcus's normal mode of operating, but he did it to help out a person in trouble.

Soon after one of the early principals of Akiba moved back to New York once his tenure was done at the school, he died very suddenly, leaving a wife and ten children. Sol Prengler told Marcus what had happened, and Marcus told him to come over in an hour. When Sol arrived, Marcus had a ten thousand–dollar check ready for the family. No one had asked Marcus to do that; no one had solicited the money. But Marcus was sympathetic to people in need, especially widows and orphans—for nearly fifty years, Marcus gave generously to Bayit LaPleitot (Girls Town Jerusalem), a girls' orphanage in Jerusalem run by Shlomo Pappenheim, a relative of Ann's.

Marcus did not publicize his generosity. He gave humbly, quietly, often anonymously to family, friends, acquaintances, and to those he did not know at all in the Dallas community and around the world.

Chapter Four

In the 1970s, Marcus's cousin, Rudy Lowy, had an occasion to sit in Marcus's office at Arrow for about half an hour. Marcus spent those thirty minutes buying and trading stocks just before their ex-dividend dates. Marcus's tactic was to buy stocks about a week before they were to declare their dividend, hold the stock, earn the distribution, and then sell the stock the next day. At that time, dividends were 85 percent tax-free. If the stock went up a certain amount before the dividend was given, he'd sell at that point and take the gain.

With only an eighth-grade education, the knowledge Marcus possessed in many different disciplines was completely self-taught. Not only did he acquire expertise on production equipment and machinery, operational efficiencies, and the like, but he could also speak proficiently with the brightest financial minds in the industry about capital markets, bonds, interest, and investments.

People respected Marcus not only at Arrow and in the Jewish community but in the non-Jewish business world in Dallas as well. At one point, Marcus was invited, along with other CEOs, to attend an exclusive presentation at the Four Seasons hotel in Irving, Texas, where Alan Greenspan, chairman of the Federal Reserve, was speaking. Marcus went and took along his daughter Helen.

As the presentation ended, Marcus turned to Helen and said, "I just don't understand it. How can this country run if the stock market is only interested in the next quarter's earnings?"

Then Marcus saw Greenspan walking by, and they started talking. Marcus expressed his confusion about the short-sighted analysis of the market in which the price of a stock is based on just one quarter's earnings or the projected earnings in the next quarter.

"What about the mid-term and long-term projections on returns," Marcus asked, "or the history of returns or the other factors?"

Greenspan was quiet for a moment, but then he said, "You know, you're right."

In the 1980s, when the real estate bubble in Texas was near its peak, Marcus would read the prospectus for various real estate deals and say, "The covenants and the projections they put on these deals will fail. It will take three years, four years, maybe five years, but they will fail."

Marcus always read the fine print and never invested a single dime in any of these real estate deals nor in the savings and loans deals that were also trendy at the time. Marcus was not greedy, nor was he a showy person. He did not lead a flashy lifestyle, wear fancy clothes, or live in an extravagant home. He outsmarted many people he dealt with, but he was always very honest in his business affairs. Marcus's main interest was in taking care of his family, his employees, and those in need.

At the same time, Marcus knew how to work with bankers and presidents of very large companies. He was well-known and highly regarded by local banks and businessmen because of his many accomplishments both inside and outside of the business world. On one occasion, a top bank chairman in Dallas brought his son, who was a high school student, over to Marcus's home in the evening. This man knew Marcus was a survivor of Auschwitz and wanted his son to learn about the Holocaust from someone who had personally endured the tragedies of that time period. Together the three men sat in Marcus's home office, surrounded by a plethora of books—mostly biographies and volumes of history—and quietly talked about the dangers that can result when decent men allow evil to take root.

Chapter Five

$\mathcal{B}$y the late 1980s, Marcus's son, Steven, was deeply entrenched at Arrow. Also during that time, David's oldest son Shelly moved back to town with his new bride and began working at Arrow. Over the next few years, Shelly's brothers, Bernie and Oscar, also returned to Dallas to embark on their careers in the family business.

Back row from left to right: Steven Rosenberg, Bernie Rosenberg, David Rosenberg
Front seated: Marcus Rosenberg

The same year Shelly started at Arrow, a major packaged foods conglomerate, ConAgra Foods Incorporated, approached Arrow Industries to see if the company had any interest in being bought out. ConAgra had been following Arrow's performance for some time, impressed by the depth of its reach into the private-label market. Arrow told ConAgra it was not looking to sell. However, Arrow's disinterest in the offer did not deter ConAgra from keeping a watchful eye on the Rosenbergs' company.

In the fall of 1991, ConAgra approached Arrow once again. While it was a very difficult decision, Marcus and David ultimately came to the conclusion that the opportunity was fortuitous and the time was right to sell.

In January of 1992, Arrow Industries ceased being a family-owned business. ConAgra took over the forty-year-old company, which at the time had 1,200 employees in Texas, Arkansas, and Tennessee, dominated the private-label business, and was the nation's largest supplier of plastic bags to the baking and ice industries.

Steven stayed on and became president of the operation in April 1992. After five years or so, he left because it became increasingly clear that ConAgra was not going to invest in the business to keep it moving forward. When all was said and done, Arrow and its business model did not fit into ConAgra's long-term strategic plan. ConAgra was a branded food company, and dealing with private labels was something it never entirely got its arms around.

Eventually, all the divisions of what had been Arrow—the foil, beans, plastics, charcoal, and so on—were either shut down or sold off to companies that had formerly been competitors of the Rosenbergs.

* ~ * ~ * ~ * ~ * ~ * ~ * ~ * ~ *

Leaving the company and adjusting to a slower pace was not easy for Marcus. One day, many hundreds of employees were reporting to him, and the next day, they weren't. He missed people coming to him, talking to him, consulting with him. He missed the everyday work, the projects, the ideas, and the challenges.

The transition to retirement was difficult for Marcus.

ARROW INDUSTRIES, INC.

January 2, 1992

TO: ALL ARROW ASSOCIATES

It is with great pride and enthusiasm that effective today, we announce the merger of Arrow Industries, Inc. with ConAgra, Inc. of Omaha, Nebraska. We believe this is an excellent fit between our two companies. ConAgra is a diversified food company comprising 160 facilities and over 75,000 employees. ConAgra's 1992 sales is expected to exceed 20 billion dollars. Many of ConAgra's brand names are well known such as Hunts Ketchup, Wesson Oil, Peter Pan Peanut Butter, La Choy Chinese Foods, Orville Redenbachers Popcorn, Healthy Choice Frozen Meals, Country Pride Chicken, Armour-Swift Meats, Butterball Turkeys, and the list goes on!

ConAgra was attracted to Arrow's strong Private Label marketing capabilities and extensive packaging operations. We anticipate that the combination of the two companies will lead to fast growth and increased earnings.

Arrow will function as an independent operating company consistent with ConAgra's corporate philosophy.

We look forward to being an integral part of the ConAgra family and are happy that our valued associates will be able to benefit from the security and opportunities presented by a large, diversified, and financially stable company such as ConAgra. We will provide further communications as the strategy between our companies develops.

We would like to extend our heartfelt appreciation to all of our associates who have worked hard these past 40 years to build our fine company. This effort has enabled us to join ConAgra and build upon the solid foundation we have established. The future looks exceedingly bright!

Best wishes to you and your families for a Happy and Prosperous New Year!

Sincerely,

Marcus Rosenberg
President and Chairman of the Board

David Rosenberg
Executive Vice President & Director

MR/jp

Arrow's letter of sale to ConAgra

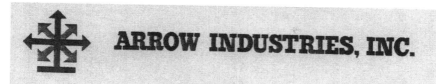

ARROW INDUSTRIES, INC.

January 27, 1992

TO: ALL ARROW ASSOCIATES

The founders of Arrow Industries, Marcus and David Rosenberg, announce their retirement effective February 3, 1992. Marcus and David founded Arrow in 1950, and grew the company to 1,200 associates, seven plants, and 185 million in sales when Arrow was merged into ConAgra earlier this year. Marcus and David have earned the admiration and respect of all Arrow associates, suppliers, and customers. We wish them the best of health and plan to continue to build upon the solid foundation they have established for us.

Marcus will assist Arrow in the transition on a consulting basis.

David will also assist in the transition on a consulting basis as well as work for Phillip Fletcher, President and Chief Operating Officer of ConAgra, Inc. to develop new private label markets for other ConAgra companies.

Retirement letter for Marcus and David Rosenberg

Chapter Six

*M*arcus's daughter Margot met Randy Pulitzer, a second-year law student, on a blind date in New York in September of 1982. After three dates, they decided to marry. Their wedding was in 1983. But before they wed, Randy first needed to meet Margot's parents. Marcus had told Randy on the phone that he had a partner and that the partner would have to agree to the marriage. That partner was Ann. So the young couple travelled to Dallas to spend a Shabbat with Ann and Marcus.

Marcus had a tendency to raid the refrigerator at nighttime. On that particular Shabbat, Randy was sleeping in the playroom in the back of the house. When he got up to get some water in the middle of the night, he happened upon Marcus in the kitchen with his head in the refrigerator, looking for something to nosh on. Marcus and Randy were both in their bedclothes. Marcus looked up at Randy, grunted a few times, shook his head, and went back to sleep. Over time, Marcus would come to love Randy as one of his own.

* ~ * ~ * ~ * ~ * ~ * ~ * ~ *

In the summer of 1991, before Sheri went to law school, she spent several months studying in Budapest. During that time, she went to see Auschwitz. Encountering the death camp in person impacted Sheri deeply. While she was in law school, her efforts were focused on many different activities related to human rights, with an emphasis on work intended to prevent future mass atrocities. Marcus had a difficult time understanding what she was trying to accomplish; he thought she should just go get a job at a law firm.

In the 1990s, when ethnic conflicts erupted in Bosnia and Kosovo, Sheri saw images on the evening news and in the newspapers that looked all too familiar, reminiscent of those from the Holocaust. In 2000, Sheri decided to take a job with the State Department and go to Bosnia to work with a quasi-international tribunal, established under the Dayton Peace Agreement. The fighting was officially over, and the war-torn country was in the beginning stages of rebuilding. Bombed-out roads, buildings, and homes defined the landscape, and people were struggling to recover emotionally and economically from the ravages of the war.

Sheri went to Bosnia to help ameliorate some of the injustices caused by discrimination. In certain towns that were controlled by the Serbs, all the Croats and Bosnians had been forced out and their properties confiscated. In towns controlled by Bosnians, the same type of treatment had been dealt to the Serbs. Serbs who lost property made claims in Bosnian courts and had their cases rejected because of ethnicity. International courts were established to handle the appeals of these cases. Sheri was involved with the courts and cases, working with the judges to write opinions and seeking to remedy the violations and damages caused by racial and national discrimination.

When she first told Marcus about her plans, he did not take the news well. He asked why she would want to put herself in a dangerous situation like that. Sheri could see only that she wanted to do whatever she could to improve the lives of those who had been victimized during a great tragedy. Marcus could see only that his daughter, a young Jewish woman, was voluntarily entering a world that had been recently plunged into barbarity like the one he had struggled to survive and overcome.

Over time, Marcus came to accept Sheri's convictions, and when she returned from her two years in Bosnia, he told her that he understood her quest for justice.

"Yes, I am looking for justice, and since it doesn't exist in its true form and can never really be found, it's not a bad business model," Sheri said.

~~*~*~*~*~*~*~*

In early 1987, Marcus's daughter Lizzy met Jules Greif in a set-up by mutual friends. About five months into the courtship, Jules came down to Dallas around Mother's Day to meet Marcus and Ann. Jules's very first encounter with Marcus was in the living room of the Rosenberg home. There Marcus was trying to connect a new Betamax recorder to his television. When he discovered that one of the connecting wires was missing, he asked Jules to go to Radio Shack with him to get what he needed.

Jules agreed, and the two of them got into Marcus's big Lincoln Town Car. As they were headed north on Preston Road, Jules noticed that Marcus was driving with both feet—one on the gas and one on the brake. Just as they got to Willow Lane, the car sputtered and stopped. Marcus looked surprised.

"Oh no, I calculated wrong," he said.

Jules turned to him and asked what he meant.

Marcus explained that, when he filled up, he would put in a certain number of gallons of gasoline. Then knowing he had a range of something like three hundred miles, he'd calculate with the odometer how many miles he would get per gallon. This methodology worked all the time for him. Except this time.

So Jules sat there, trying to figure out if Marcus knew what to do next. Unsure if running out of gas was a common occurrence, Jules asked him where the nearest gas station was. Marcus told him it was just up the road, at the corner of Preston and LBJ Freeway. Of course, Jules had no idea how far away that actually was when he offered to push the car down the road while Marcus steered. At first, Jules was pushing and pushing; then noticing they were not getting anywhere, he told Marcus to put the car in neutral. Jules was soaked through his clothes after only five minutes of shoving Marcus's boat of a car down Preston Road. It was a very warm spring day in Dallas.

A policeman saw them and helped by diverting some of the traffic. He had them push the car into a parking lot just past Harvest Hill next to a bank. Then they walked the rest of the way to the gas station, got a gas can, and filled it up. All the while, Jules was thinking to himself, *I really like Lizzy, but do I really like her that much?*

Marcus would come to love Jules as one of his own.

* ⁓ * ⁓ * ⁓ * ⁓ * ⁓ * ⁓ * ⁓ *

Marcus's children began marrying and starting families of their own. Helen married Willy Waks, and they had three children: David, Daniel, and Noa. In later years, Helen remarried Shami Waldman. Steven married Ruthy Fogel, and they also had three children: Elie, Ariela, and Dana. Margot married Randy Pulitzer, and they had four children: Jessica, Samuel, Miles, and Mina. Lizzy married Jules Greif, and they had two children: Gabriella and Jake. A number of years later, Sheri married Gregg Kanter, and they had three children: Markus, Maurice, and Margaux.

Marcus with his grandson, Miles Pulitzer

Marcus loved his grandchildren very much and showered attention on them whenever he could. They called Ann *Oma* and Marcus *Opa*. The grandchildren were given nicknames by Marcus: Miles was "Smiles," Ariela was "Cinderella," Jake was "Jukey," and so on. A big bowl of KitKat bars—or "kitty cat bars," as Marcus would call them—was always waiting for the children in Marcus's hiding place at the top of the closet in his office at home.

Marcus and Ann Rosenberg with their grandchildren Mina Pulitzer
and Jake Greif at the Akiba Academy (Churchill Way) playground

David Waks was one of Marcus's oldest grandchildren, and the two
of them had an easy, natural, close relationship from the very beginning.
Like Marcus's children, David would sometimes go to Arrow on Sunday
mornings with Marcus. Young David absolutely adored these outings with
his opa. He also loved seeing the trucks, trailers, and forklifts at the plant.
On one of his first visits to Arrow, when he was around four years old,
David looked up at his grandfather and said, "Opa, you are really, really
rich! You have all these big trucks to play with!" David could never get
enough of those trucks.

In the summer of 1998, Marcus invited two of his grandsons, David
and Elie, on a Bar Ilan delegation trip commemorating the one hundredth
anniversary of the first Zionist Congress held in Basel, Switzerland back
in 1898. The trip was a Bar Mitzvah gift for Elie, who was thirteen, and
an early Bar Mitzvah gift for David, who was one year younger than his
cousin.

This delegation went to Prague and Basel, where Marcus's daughter
Helen met up with them, and then they went on to Israel. The delegates

on the tour enjoyed having the boys around; they livened things up. But for Marcus, the many cocktail parties and continual socializing were too much; he ended up spending even more time with the boys than originally planned. The two grandsons especially enjoyed their time together in Prague and hearing Marcus's perspectives on historical events in the region. Though he easily could have, Marcus did not take his grandsons to Bardejov, the place of his youth. Marcus would not go back to his hometown on that trip or at any other time in his life. He was very private about what had happened to him in the old country, and the two boys were too young to know how to broach the subject.

Marcus in Prague with other delegates of the Bar Ilan mission

When David went off to college, he was very diligent about keeping in touch with Marcus on a weekly basis. And when he came home to visit, he always made a point of seeing his grandfather and having lunch with him. Sometimes, they would spend hours together watching comedies on TV. And Marcus always appreciated the gag gifts David gave to him for birthdays and Chanukah. David was by far the most engaged of the grandchildren with Marcus. The grandfather and grandson had a uniquely wonderful connection.

~~*~*~*~*~*~*~*

At the end of December 1998, Marcus's daughter Margot was diagnosed with breast cancer. She went through the recommended rounds of chemotherapy and radiation, and after her treatments were completed, the doctor said her cancer was gone. He then told her she had a 97-percent chance of remaining in remission for the rest of her life.

Chapter Seven

 ⟨✦⟩

As Shaare Tefilla grew, so did philosophical differences within the institution. Toward the end of 1999, the synagogue split. Moshe Levy took over the presidency again at the shul, helping to ensure that the transition after the split would go as smoothly as possible.

Similar philosophical differences were taking place at Akiba Academy, and toward the beginning of the 2002-2003 school year, the school also underwent a split.

During the tumultuous times leading up to the split of the shul, Marcus had a number of lunches with one of his close friends. In those get-togethers, Marcus opened up and expressed his concerns about what was happening. He would say, "How do these guys just come into town and try to turn the whole thing upside down?"

He told his friend that it was fine if they wanted something different. They were welcome to go somewhere else and start their own institutions. But Marcus felt that they should not be trying to take over an existing shul and change its direction.

Marcus lamented the disharmony that had overtaken the Dallas Orthodox world. He had worked hard to revive and build Orthodoxy in Dallas, despite tremendous apathy from the community at the time. And during those years, he said he always had room for others who didn't necessarily see the world as he did—as long as the person was decent, upstanding, and honest. Pluralism and collegiality within the community were very important to Marcus. He sought to welcome incoming professionals to Dallas, feeling the city needed strong leaders in all strands of Judaism in order for the community to be alive with possibilities and flourish.

What hurt Marcus most about the break in the community was that, during the events that led up to the split, he had been made to feel that there no longer was a place for him or for what he had built. Even though Marcus believed his institutions were still vital and relevant, he confided in his friend that he felt deeply betrayed.

Around the time that Akiba was going through the process of splitting, Leslie and Howard Schultz purchased Olla Podrida, a crafts mall that had closed down in 1986. The former mall sat on nearly eight and a half acres, and the Schultzes had plans to donate the land so that Akiba could build a new home on the site. In addition, the hope was that Yavneh Academy would also be housed in its first permanent facility on the property.

Both school boards held a vote on whether or not to move to a shared campus, and both boards passed the motion. With the split behind them and Akiba and Yavneh headed to a brand new campus, the community looked toward the future with renewed optimism.

In 1999, a community capital campaign in Dallas was established to help ten member organizations of the Jewish Federation make capital improvements. The construction of the new campus for Akiba and Yavneh became part of the campaign. Around the time of the Akiba split, the leaders of the Akiba-Yavneh campus capital campaign needed to make decisions about how big the campus would be and how the project would be funded.

Before they could reach any resolutions in this regard, it was necessary for Marcus to commit to how much money he was going to donate. Howard and Leslie Schultz were determined to see the new campus built and had already invested a huge sum of money. But those dollars, along with the capital campaign funding, still were insufficient. Many millions more were needed.

A group of community leaders led by Steven Rosenberg met with Marcus at his home. Richard Rohan was there, as was David Agronin, the CEO of the Dallas Jewish Community Foundation. As the group began talking, Marcus voiced his concerns about the campus. Based upon the proposed designs he'd seen, Marcus felt the project was going to be a very expensive proposition. How were the schools going to pay for it? Where was the money coming from? He thought it was a beautiful concept, but he feared the schools would reach a point where they would not be able to operate the campus efficiently.

The meeting lasted about two hours, and everyone left without resolution, except David Agronin. David stayed at the house because he believed that, beneath all the concerns and protests, Marcus really was interested in becoming a cofounder of this new project. The two men talked about many things that afternoon. Marcus spoke about Ann and how she was the one who had originally wanted a Jewish school in Dallas. He mentioned Hillel Academy, the first day school in the city. He went on to tell the story about Agudas Achim and the founding years of Akiba. And he talked at length about the split of Shaare Tefilla.

Then, after five hours of conversation, Marcus told David what he had been hoping to hear—that Marcus would like his name on the new campus. Marcus spoke about his gratitude to Howard Schultz and how Marcus had brought Howard into the school because he was very impressed with him and his potential to lead Akiba. He admired the fact that Howard and Leslie's children attended Akiba and was very pleased with the role the Schultz family had played at the school. Marcus greatly respected their generosity. And Marcus wanted the Rosenberg name to be next to the Schultz name on the campus—not for himself but for his children. Marcus wanted his offspring to have a constant reminder of their responsibility to support the school financially. He wished for his grandchildren to understand that they were part of this legacy as well and equally accountable for the institution's sustainability. This was the only way he knew how to ensure that they would commit to that responsibility when Marcus was gone.

David told Marcus that Howard wanted his family name on the

campus for the same reasons and that, if Marcus wanted his name next to Howard's, he would have to talk to Howard about it. Marcus needed to understand that the naming would be coupled with a cost. Howard had already committed many millions of dollars, but many millions more were still needed. Marcus said he had already put in money with an endowment to Akiba, Yavneh, and Shaare Tefilla. More money was coming, and additional funds were set up in his will for the institutions. David again encouraged Marcus to talk to Howard about specific numbers. When David left Marcus's home that evening, he phoned Howard to tell him what had transpired.

The next morning, Howard and Marcus met to have coffee and talk about the campus. They discussed the terms, and Howard went back to his family with the proposal. Though ground had not yet been broken, the building project was well underway, and Marcus was coming in later in the game. Still, the Schultz family had the highest regard for Marcus and all he had done as founder of the school. Over the course of the next few days, a deal was made, and the Schultz Rosenberg campus became a reality.

Groundbreaking of the Schultz Rosenberg campus in 2004
From left to right: Marcus Rosenberg, Ann Rosenberg, Howard
Schultz, Leslie Schultz, Adina Romaner, Dalya Romaner
Courtesy of Holly Kuper Photography

Schultz Rosenberg Campus welcome sign
Courtesy of Holly Kuper Photography

Schultz Rosenberg Campus administrative building
Courtesy of Holly Kuper Photography

Chapter Eight

❧

The summer of 2000 was exceedingly hot. Right around Labor Day, Marcus had a stroke. The apoplexy happened at night, but Marcus did not go to the hospital, nor did he call anyone at the time. He didn't realize the gravity of the situation until he noticed in the morning that he was having problems moving. He phoned his son-in-law Jules, a pediatrician by profession. After Marcus explained what had happened, Jules called Marcus's doctor so he could meet Jules and Marcus in the emergency room.

Marcus had been a smoker for decades and had had high blood pressure for years. It was apparent to the doctors in the emergency room that Marcus had suffered a stroke. He was admitted to the hospital.

The family members all took turns staying in the hospital with him; he was never alone. With a good, calming energy, Margot was especially caring and nurturing. Marcus had always held a very special place in his heart for her. During those weeks she was watching over him, she began to limp. She blamed it on her new trainer. Maybe she had pulled a groin muscle. Whatever the reason, she was in a lot of pain, but she put off checking into it because she was busy helping her father.

When Marcus was released from the hospital, Margot finally made an appointment with her doctor. A series of tests were run, and she had to meet with her physician to find out the results. Erev Rosh Hashana was the earliest appointment she could get for the follow-up visit. Sheri drove

Margot to the doctor's office that day and was by her sister's side when Margot was told that regretfully she was in the 3 percent and not the 97 percent—her cancer had returned and metastasized into her bones. The doctor told her that, this time, the disease would take her life, and she had anywhere from three months to ten years to live. She would start another regimen of chemotherapy to try to slow the cancer's progress, but basically, Margot had just received her death sentence.

With heavy hearts, she and Sheri went home to tell their family. That night, everyone was at the house for Rosh Hashana. Marcus got up to make kiddush, and halfway through the blessing, he broke down and started crying. Stumbling into his office down the hall, he said he couldn't handle it. He thought the Holocaust had stolen all the loved ones he was to lose. The thought of another personal tragedy was unbearable.

Despite the chemotherapy, Margot's health continued to decline. For a while, she was on crutches. When she no longer had the strength to use those, she went into a wheelchair.

During those fleeting weeks and months, Marcus spoke to Rabbi Wolk. Another woman at the school had suffered from breast cancer at the same time that Margot's had been first discovered. Yet, this other woman's cancer had not returned, while Margot's had.

Marcus turned to Wolk and said, "Look, two women, the same illness, the same kind of treatment: one it works for, one it doesn't. All the money in the world, and I can't help Margot."

At the end, Margot spent her last days in the hospital. When Marcus's sister's husband, Andy, had had his three open-heart surgeries, Marcus had always been there, every single time, sitting in the waiting room with Erika, offering her comfort. But Marcus could not bring himself to see Margot in the hospital. Some family members had a hard time comprehending why, but in the end, he was simply unable to watch his beloved daughter die. Jules understood that every person has his or her own way of dealing with loss.

Margot passed on the morning of January 21, 2002. At her funeral, no emotion could be seen on Marcus's face. He was completely silent, much in the way that the biblical Aaron was silent when his two sons, Nadav and Avihu, were struck down. Marcus wept on the inside, and he wept for Margot the rest of his life.

Margot Rosenberg Pulitzer and Marcus Rosenberg

The music building at Bar Ilan took on Margot's name as did the endowments Marcus set up for Akiba, Yavneh, and Shaare Tefilla.

Chapter Nine

After his stroke, Marcus stopped smoking; he never lit a cigarette again. His mobility was greatly limited, yet he refused to go into a wheelchair.

Isai was the one who really helped him through this difficult period. Isai Carcamo began working for the Rosenbergs in 1987 when he was still a teenager. His aunt had been an employee in the Rosenberg home for thirty-seven years. When she passed away in 1989, Isai took her place. In the beginning, Isai didn't speak much English, but as he learned the language, he developed more of a relationship with Marcus.

One day when Isai was nineteen, Marcus took him to the nursery to pick out some flowers to plant in the backyard. When Isai was done with his work, Marcus paid him sixty dollars. Isai was elated; he had never made that much money in his entire life.

When Marcus had his stroke, Isai became his full-time assistant. They'd go out to eat, check out Marcus's warehouses and real estate properties, and visit Marcus's lawyer, accountant, and broker. Together they would go to the Tom Thumb grocery store around the corner just to look around and see what was happening. Isai cooked some for Marcus, but Marcus was actually the better chef. Marcus was very comfortable in the kitchen, and everything he cooked turned out well. He especially enjoyed preparing fish. Marcus never got mad at Isai. And whenever he wanted Isai to do something, he didn't say, "You need to do this" or "You need to do that."

Rather Marcus would say, "I'll tell you what we're going to do ..." Isai appreciated Marcus's honesty and straightforwardness.

The two men talked at length about religion. Isai's faith was interesting to Marcus. He was a member of Apostolic and Prophets, which is similar to the Mennonite religion. While not very well-known in Texas, Apostolic and Prophets has a large following in South America. In religious services, the men sit on one side of the sanctuary, and the women sit on the other. When a child is born, the baby is presented at the temple after thirty-three days. And the people of this faith believe that the Jews are the people God chose.

Marcus spent a lot of time at home after his stroke, and while he kept up with the news of the world and how the financial markets were affecting his investments, he also wanted to learn how to use the computer. A team of experts—his grandsons Elie and David, as well as Isai—were at his beck and call. They would try to teach him about Microsoft Office and other applications. Marcus would get annoyed with himself because he wasn't picking up the concepts as fast as he'd like. His grandsons took note that, while their grandfather struggled to gain expertise on the computer, he had been at the forefront of investing in companies such as Microsoft, Dell, and the like in the early 1990s. Though he never mastered how to populate a database, Marcus had a very keen sense of what was going to take off and make money in the world of technology.

He did learn how to use e-mail, and one of his favorite aspects of electronic mail was receiving jokes. Marcus told a few of his favorite jokes over and over again to Isai. One of them went as follows:

A guy coming to the United States from Europe is trying to smuggle in some gold. The way he does this is by encasing the gold into seven sets of dentures. When he goes through customs, he's asked why he needs so many sets of dentures.

The guy says, "Well, one is for when I eat meat. The second is for when I eat dairy. And the third one is for when I eat *pareve* food."

The security guard says, "Well, that's only three sets. What about the others?"

So the guy replies, "Well, it's the same thing, except for Passover: one is for meat; one is for dairy; one is for pareve."

"Okay," the security guard says, "but that still leaves one set of dentures. What are those for?"

"Oh, those? Those are for when I want to eat something *treif.*"

During these times, Marcus also enjoyed watching sports on TV, especially soccer and boxing. If the Czech teams were playing in any games, Marcus and Manny always rooted for them. But if Slovakia was in a competition, the two brothers spat at the TV.

In January 2002, Marcus's dear friend, Sol Prengler passed away.

From left to right: Marcus Rosenberg, Sol Prengler

That same year, Marcus started a Torah study group at his home. Over the course of the next two to three years, two new rabbis in Dallas,

Rabbi Ari Perl and Rabbi Meir Tannenbaum, led the bimonthly Monday lunchtime learning. Ronnie Gruen, Sol Schwartz, and Manny joined Marcus in his class.

Marcus especially enjoyed studying business topics because they were infused with uniquely Jewish ethics. He appreciated Judaism's focus on "Seller Beware" rather than "Buyer Beware" and liked discussions related to practical life, business acumen, and business experience—topics such as laws of interest, advertising, competition, and boundaries of infringement. These were the matters he had learned about as a boy in cheder, values very much engrained in him.

In the tractate *Bava Batra*, a concept called *hasagat gevul* speaks about established markets and the kind of consideration given to someone else coming in, opening a similar store, and engaging in competition. Business owners have some protection from having their business taken away. On the other hand, Judaism subscribes to the notions of competition and a free-market system. An interesting tension is seen in this aspect of Jewish law. The laws related to hasagat gevul were the ones that most interested Marcus more than half a century earlier when he was a *talmid chacham* in Bardejov. In this new study group, he brought up certain *mishnayot* he had learned sixty years before in cheder; he even still remembered some passages by heart.

Because the men in the study group had already experienced life on so many different levels, discussing these types of laws gave them an opportunity to contrast various economic systems such as socialism and capitalism. Each of them had European roots, and the discussions became very interesting and lively. Manny and Marcus especially were not big fans of the socialist model. They spoke highly of how well they had thrived under capitalism and the free-market system, appreciating all the opportunities they had been given. To the facilitating rabbis of the class, these older gentlemen's perspectives were wonderfully unique and insightful.

Each class, the rabbi would prepare a source sheet on a particular topic, introduce what they were going to be learning, and then step back as the group began discussing, talking, and arguing amongst themselves. Each man's individual life experiences and outlooks came into play during these discussions.

Marcus was the hard-core businessman who was thinking about these topics from an almost purely business standpoint. Manny liked to invoke his legal background and bring in concepts from secular law to talk about which approach he favored. Ronnie was the social conscience, the artist of the group, who talked about aesthetics. Sol was the intellectual philosopher. The dynamic between them was intriguing and oftentimes entertaining.

Sometimes when they conversed, an appreciation for each other's perspectives was somewhat lacking. It wasn't uncommon for a conversation to end with one or more of the men intoning a decisive and time-honored, "Echhh ...

After his stroke, Marcus greatly disliked being alone. When Ann was not home, he always invited people over—friends, grandchildren, whoever would stay and be with him. He wanted Isai with him at all times.

Whenever Marcus went out of the house, Isai was there. Marcus held on to him for balance, but if Marcus came across someone he knew, he would push Isai away. He never wanted to show the outside world any signs of weakness or be seen as a frail old man.

Helen's son Daniel was at a family simcha some years after Marcus's stroke. Everyone was milling about the kiddush hall, eating and socializing. However, Marcus was too tired to get up from his chair. Daniel came by to talk to him for a minute, and as he got up to leave, Marcus touched his grandson's arm and said, "Sit, sit, sit, sit, sit ..." He did not want to be alone. Daniel returned to his chair and tried to make conversation with his grandfather. But Marcus was too weary to respond.

What began as cardiovascular disease moved into renal failure. Marcus was told by his doctor that he would die unless he began dialysis. Marcus looked into his options. The type of treatment he needed would require him to spend every other day hooked up to a dialysis machine for six to eight hours. The day after each treatment, he would be totally exhausted. Only one day a week would he skip the process, meaning, only one day a week would he feel well. Marcus decided this was not for him. The way he figured it, he had lived sixty years longer than he should have. His life had been full, and he was not going to spend his last years hooked up to a machine. Just as he had chosen his path in life, he chose his path for exiting this world. Marcus always liked things done on his own terms.

⁓⁓*⁓*⁓*⁓*⁓*⁓*⁓*

On Monday, February 13, 2005, Marcus was not feeling well and cancelled his weekly Torah class. Two days later, Isai noticed that Marcus looked very weak. On that day, Isai was going to the store to buy some walkie-talkies so that he and Marcus could communicate around the house when Isai was not in Marcus's immediate vicinity. Marcus had never asked Isai to help him get from his bedroom to the office, but on that day he did. A little later, he told Isai he was having trouble breathing. Ann was at the school attending a program for her granddaughter Gabriella Greif, so Isai called for an ambulance to come for Marcus.

Once Marcus was admitted into the hospital, his condition deteriorated rapidly. Isai came the next morning to bring Marcus's reading glasses, but at that point, Marcus no longer recognized his friend. He went into a coma-like state, and everyone knew the end was near.

Helen called her son David, who was in school in Philadelphia, and told him to get a flight back to Dallas as soon as possible. It had been snowing all day in Philly, and his flight out was delayed two hours. He arrived in Atlanta just in time to see his connecting plane pull out of the gate. David was in agony, because he knew he would have to wait until the next morning to get another flight to Dallas. He prayed over and over that Opa would hang on until he got to the hospital.

In the meantime, his brother Daniel knew what David was going through. Though he was not as close with his grandfather as David was, he asked his mother if he could stay the night in the hospital with Marcus. He was doing it for David, because he could not be there—David was one of Marcus's best friends; they were unbelievably close. Helen reluctantly agreed to Daniel being David's surrogate that night.

Ann and Lizzy were in the hospital that evening as well.

Daniel kept going over to Marcus and saying, "Hang in there, Opa. David's on his way. He'll be here soon."

Ann went to sleep on a cot in the room, and Lizzy was on the bed next to her. Only Daniel was awake. He kept an eye on Marcus and his breathing machine. His breathing was inconsistent—on and off, a break every now and then, very labored. This went on for some time. All of a sudden, Daniel couldn't hear Marcus breathing anymore. The machine had flat-lined, and Daniel burst down the hall to find a nurse.

"Something stopped! Something stopped," he screamed.

A nurse went into the room, took a look at Marcus, and said, "Yes, we lost him. Please inform your family." Then she went to get a doctor.

Daniel tapped his grandmother on the shoulder and whispered, "Oma ... Oma ... I'm sorry. He's gone."

Ann jumped off the cot and went over to Marcus. She gazed at him for a few moments, reached out with her hand to close his eyes, and then softly kissed her husband good-bye.

Marcus and Ann Rosenberg in Washington, DC

Ann and Marcus Rosenberg

Marcus Abraham Rosenberg passed into the next world on Friday, February 18, 2005.

David boarded the six a.m. flight from Atlanta to Dallas. When his plane landed, he turned on his cell phone and was surprised to see he'd received a large number of voice messages, each one, as it turned out, a condolence call on the loss of his grandfather. The grandchild who was so incredibly close to Marcus was not able to be with him when he died. But he was there for the funeral, and he did sit with his grandfather's body in the funeral home before the burial.

On the cold, sunny Sunday morning of February 20, 2005, Marcus was laid to rest. Many family members spoke at the service, offering insightful words about Marcus and his life. Both Rabbi Wolk, the first rabbi of Shaare Tefilla, and Rabbi Perl, Wolk's successor, spoke as well.

Rabbi Wolk talked about Marcus's gift to the city of Dallas—the gift of enabling the transmission of Torah. He said that Marcus knew the only way to ensure the survival of future generations was through the continued study of Judaism's holy texts. Both the teacher of Torah and the one who facilitates the study of Torah help strengthen and maintain God's world.

"Marcus enabled scores, hundreds, thousands of boys and girls through the years to study Torah," Rabbi Wolk said. "He enabled them to study God's world through math and science. Every *passuk* of Chumash, every *blatt* of gemara can be traced back to Marcus's dedication. He understood that, without Jewish education, a spiritual devastation would befall our people. He did not want to see that. One devastation was all he could experience."

When Rabbi Perl spoke, he likened Marcus to Judaism's forefather, Jacob, who planted trees on the outskirts of Egypt while on his way to reunite with his son, Joseph: "The Midrash speaks of this act firstly as Jacob's innate ability to envision the future and recognize the needs of future generations. And secondly, the act is a tribute to the selflessness of Jacob's actions, planting trees whose fruit he would never taste.

"Like our forefather Jacob, Mr. Rosenberg had an incredible capacity to envision the future of our community long before some were ready for his vision and even in the face of those who actively opposed it. And like our forefather Jacob, when Mr. Rosenberg planted trees, it wasn't so that he could taste the fruit himself. Marcus Rosenberg planted for his children, for his grandchildren, and for the Jewish people.

"The trees he planted were for us, the Jewish community of Dallas.

"The trees he planted were for the Jewish people in the United States, in Israel, and around the world.

"But the trees this great man planted were never, ever planted for Marcus Rosenberg.

"As we partake of the beautiful fruits borne of his remarkable life, he will never, ever be forgotten.

"May his soul be bound up in the bonds of eternal life."

Dear Ann,

I was so sorry to learn about Marcus from Linda. Although we traveled together so long ago, I always felt that both of you were exceptional people and that if we lived closer and saw each other more, we would have been good friends.

Marcus was so smart and really understood how important it is for us to take care of our fellow Jews when they are in trouble. You were fortunate to be married to such an exceptional and visionary person.

You have my deepest condolences.

Yours Truly,
Jane

Thinking of you
during this time of sorrow.

Our Deepest Sympathy
Jane & Stuart Weitzman

Translation of Hebrew: "He who brings peace to His universe will bring peace to u and to all the people Israel, and let us say, Amen."
the last line of the Mourners' Kaddish

Condolence letter from Jane and Stuart Weitzman,
friends of Marcus and Ann Rosenberg

Afterword

⟨✦⟩

At the time of the writing of this book, Marcus had a legacy of fifteen grandchildren (two of them married) and two great-grandchildren, with hopes of many more to come, God willing.

The institutions he founded, along with those he gave generously to, continue to advance and thrive.

Front row, from left to right: Miles Pulitzer, Ann Rosenberg, David Waks
Middle row, from left to right: Elie Rosenberg, Shalva Rosenberg,
Tali Rosenberg, Gabriella Greif, Noa Waks, Mina Pulitzer
Back row, from left to right: Jake Greif, Daniel Waks

Marcus Rosenberg

For I have given you a good teaching, do not forsake My Torah. It is a tree of life for those who grasp it, and its supporters are praiseworthy. Its ways are ways of pleasantness and all its pathways are peace. -Proverbs 3:17-18, 4:2

240

Acknowledgments

❧

$\mathcal{I}$ would like to thank Carol Agronin, Linda Blasnik, Dia Epstein, Gregg Kanter, Sheri Rosenberg Kanter, Robert Liener, Audree Meyer, Ann Rosenberg, Ruth Sacks, and Rabbi Zev Silver, who all helped proofread and edit drafts of this book at various stages of the project.

Thanks to Asriel Agronin, Meyer Denn, Emil Fish, Ed Gaudreault, Brandon Hurtado, Holly Kuper, Charlie Lewie, Malkie Rosenberg Ozeri, Randy Pulitzer, Richard Rohan, Ann Rosenberg, Diane Siegel, Joe Torres, Gerray West, and David Zoller for help with scanning and/or providing photographs and various articles and documents.

Special thanks to Flora Robin for her helping identify so many of the faces from old Akiba Academy photos.

Thanks to Manny Rohan (z"l) and Steven Rosenberg for making available a number of family artifacts, including a variety of articles, letters, and passports.

And a final thank you to my husband and family for their constant love and support.

Glossary

afikomen. The matzo broken in the early stages of the Passover seder and set aside to be eaten as the dessert. The broken matzo is hidden so it can be found by the children.

alef beis. The Hebrew alphabet.

Aron kodesh. The ornamental receptacle that contains an institution's Torah scrolls.

ashkenazi. A Jewish descendant of French, German, or Eastern European ancestry.

ba'al tefilla. The leader of a prayer service.

baraisa. A teaching or tradition in Jewish oral law that is not incorporated in the six orders of the Mishnah.

Bar Mitzvah. Jewish coming-of-age ritual; a Jewish male who has reached the age of thirteen.

Bava Basra/Bava Batra. A tractate of talmud dealing with business law.

behelfer. An assistant to the Rabbi at a cheder.

Beis Yaakov. An Orthodox school for Jewish girls.

Birkat Hamazon. Blessings/grace after meals.

blatt. Page.

brachos/brachot. Blessings.

Chabad. A Chasidic movement known for its extensive outreach in Jewish communities throughout the world.

challah. Special braided bread eaten on the Jewish Sabbath and holidays.

chazzan. A musician trained to lead Jewish congregational prayer.

chazzanos. The art and skills of cantorial singing.

cheder. An Orthodox school for Jewish boys.

chevra. A group of friends.

Chevra Kaddisha. An organization that prepares bodies for Jewish burial.

chol hamoed. Intermediate days of the festivals of Sukkot and Passover.

Chumash. The first five books of the Jewish scriptures.

d'var Torah. A speech or lesson on a portion of Torah.

daven. To pray.

Divrei Chaim. Moniker of Rabbi Chaim Halberstam, a famous Hasidic rebbe and founder of the Sanz Hasidic dynasty.

dvrei. A cry.

Eretz Yisrael. The land of Israel.

erev. The eve of Shabbat or a Jewish holiday.

eruv. A ritual enclosure constructed in traditional Jewish communities as a means to carry objects from one domain to another on Shabbat. Without this enclosure, observant Jews would be forbidden by Jewish law from carrying any objects from indoors to a public domain.

gabbai. A person who plays a role in the Torah service, calling up congregants to read from the Torah.

gemara. A component of the Talmud composed of rabbinical analysis and commentary of the Mishnah.

get. Jewish divorce document.

Halacha. The collective body of Jewish law.

hasagat gevul. Economic competition in Jewish law.

Hashem. A Jewish name for God.

Hasidism. A branch of Judaism that promotes spirituality and joy, along with a devotion to both the revealed and hidden aspects of the Torah.

Hlinka Garda. The Hlinka party's military arm for internal security.

kapo. A Jewish prisoner in a concentration camp who was assigned by the Nazis to supervise his fellow Jews.

kashrus/kashrut. The set of Jewish dietary laws.

kiddush. (1) Ceremonial blessing over wine for the Jewish Sabbath and holidays. (2) A meal served at a synagogue after Shabbat or holiday services.

kippa. A small round cap worn by Jewish men.

l'chaim. A toast when having a drink, literally meaning "to life."

lekash. Honey cake.

mavoi. A narrow street enclosed on three sides; a cul-du-sac.

mazel tov. A congratulatory wish.

melamed. A teacher.

mikveh. A body of water used for ritual immersion in Judaism.

minyan. A quorum of ten Jewish adults needed to conduct communal prayer services.

Mishnah. The first major written version of the Jewish oral tradition.

mishnayos/mishnayot. Specific paragraphs or verses in the Mishnah.

mizrach. The direction Jews in the diaspora turn toward during prayer so they will be facing Jerusalem.

Mizrachi. A religious Zionist movement.

Modeh Ani. The first prayer of the day that a Jew recites upon awakening.

mussaf. The additional prayer service recited on Shabbat and holidays.

netilas yadayim. Ritual washing of hands.

nosh. A snack; to snack.

nusach. The style and melody of a prayer service.

parasha. A section of Torah read in Jewish prayer services.

pareve. A neutral food, neither meat nor dairy.

passuk. A sentence in the Torah.

Pesach. The Jewish holiday of Passover, commemorating the Exodus, where the ancient Israelites were freed from slavery in Egypt.

peyos. Sidelocks or sidecurls worn by many Orthodox Jewish males.

rav/rebbe. Rabbi.

Rosh Hashana. The holiday celebrating the Jewish new year.

schmooze. To make small talk or chat.

schreiber. A scribe or secretary; one who performs administrative work.

seder. A Jewish ritual feast marking the beginning of the holiday of Pesach.

sefer Torah. A handwritten copy of the Torah; a Torah scroll.

Shabbos/Shabbat. The Jewish Sabbath.

shacharit. The daily morning prayer service.

"Shalom Aleichem." The traditional song sung Friday night at the beginning of the Shabbat meal.

Shir Hamalot. Psalm 126, Song of Ascents, which is recited before Birkat Hamazon on Shabbat and Jewish holidays.

shul. Synagogue.

simcha. A happy, festive occasion.

Simchat Torah. The Jewish holiday marking the conclusion of the annual cycle of public Torah reading and the beginning of a new cycle.

s'micha. Rabbinical ordination.

sukkah. A walled structure used during the holiday of Sukkot that is intended to remind Jews of the fragile dwellings the Israelites lived in during their forty years of wandering in the desert.

Sukkos/Sukkot. The Jewish Feast of Booths.

talmid chacham. A wise student.

tefillin. A set of small black leather boxes containing scrolls of parchment inscribed with verses from the Torah; worn by observant Jews during weekday morning services.

treif. Food that is not kosher.

tzedakah. Charity and philanthropic acts.

tzumazal chumash. A small ceremony celebrating a young student's mastery over a Torah concept.

upsherin. A ritual haircut ceremony held when a Jewish boy turns three years old.

Va'ad Hakashrus. An agency certifying and supervising kashrut.

wunderkind. A child prodigy.

yahrtzeit. The anniversary of the day of death.

yiddishkeit. Jewishness; Jewish essence.

Yom Kippur. Day of Atonement, the holiest and most solemn day of the Jewish year.

Yom HaShoah. Holocaust Remembrance Day.

zmiros/zmirot. Songs sung around the table during Shabbat and holiday meals.

Sources and References

꩜

*M*y deep gratitude goes to the following individuals who made themselves available to be interviewed, some on multiple occasions:

Family/Old Country
1. Ariela Rosenberg Brafman
2. Emil Fish
3. Jack Garfein
4. Gabriella Greif
5. Jake Greif
6. Dr. Jules Greif
7. Lizzy Rosenberg Greif
8. Gregg Kanter
9. Sheri Rosenberg Kanter
10. Etsy Kogut
11. Reuben Kogut
12. Frances Leanse
13. Rudy Lowy
14. Gita Nagel
15. Jack Nagel
16. Shirley Pollack
17. Jessica Pulitzer
18. Miles Pulitzer
19. Mina Pulitzer

20. Randy Pulitzer
21. Sam Pulitzer
22. Bandi (Rosenwaser) Roberts
23. Manny Rohan z"l
24. Richard Rohan
25. Terri Rohan
26. Valle Rohan
27. Ann Rosenberg
28. Bernie Rosenberg
29. Dana Rosenberg
30. David Rosenberg
31. Elie Rosenberg
32. Gussie Rosenberg
33. Steven Rosenberg
34. Ralph Seelig
35. Shirley Seelig
36. Irwin Schmutter
37. Norman Shmutter
38. Andy Sigel
39. Dina Sigel
40. Erika Sigel
41. Gary Sigel
42. David Waks
43. Daniel Waks
44. Helen Rosenberg Waks Waldman
45. Noa Waks

Arrow

1. Gorda Baten
2. Arnold Bier
3. Gregg Brashear
4. Mike Campbell
5. Marc Cantrell
6. Michael Conway
7. Bill DeArmand

8. Russ Fondren
9. Roberta Frohardt
10. Lionel Goldstein
11. Gregg Hanson
12. Jozef Levi
13. Rosa Levi
14. Charlie Lewie
15. Jack Mimms
16. Larry Schectman
17. Victor Trubitt
18. John Wright
19. Michael Zucker

Akiba Academy

1. Rabbi Mendel Bernstein
2. Ethel Gruen
3. Carol Ann Hoppenstein
4. Hanna Lambert
5. Raymond Lambert
6. Erv Rovinsky
7. Shirley Rovinsky
8. Howard Schultz
9. Leslie Schultz
10. Bonnie Whitman

Congregation Shaare Tefilla

1. Dr. Paul Chafetz
2. Jeff Fine
3. Dr. Moshe Levi
4. David Radunsky
5. Dr. Max Ribald
6. David Wohlstadter
7. Marilyn Wohlstadter
8. Rabbi Howard Wolk

Community/Friends

1. David Agronin
2. Matthew Berke
3. Rachel Berke
4. Helen Biderman
5. Isai Carcamo
6. Rabbi Yitzchak Cohen
7. Rabbi Mendel Dubrawsky
8. Walter Levy
9. Rabbi Ari Perl
10. Herschel Prengler
11. Dan Prescott
12. Sol Schwartz
13. Zella Sober z"l
14. Moe Stein
15. Rabbi Meir Tannenbaum
16. Sarah Weinschneider
17. Rabbi Sidney Weinschneider
18. Rabbi Stewart Weiss
19. Marilynn Wohlstadter
20. Michael Wolfson
21. Rabbi Sheldon Zimmerman

References

Akiba Academy of Dallas. 1966. "Akiba Academy Building Campaign. "

Akiba Academy of Dallas. 1968. "New Building Dedication Program. "

Akiba Academy of Dallas. 1992. "Akiba Academy 30th Anniversary Civic Service Dinner Journal."

Arrow. 1956, 1964, 1972."Articles of Incorporation." Austin, TX: Secretary of State, Business and Public Filings Division.

ArtScroll Mesorah Series. 1990. *The Complete Artscroll Siddur.* Brooklyn, New York: Mesorah Publications, Ltd.

Fuchs, Abraham. 1998. *The Unheeded Cry.* Brooklyn, NY: Mesorah Publications, Ltd.

Grussgott, Avrum. 1988. *Bardejov Remembered: A Memorial to the Jewish Community of Bardejov, Czechoslovakia 1734-1945.* Brooklyn, NY.

Jacobs, Ginger (facilitator). circa 1990. "Marcus Rosenberg: Jewish Day Schools of Dallas." Audio visual presentation of a panel discussion. Dallas, TX: Jewish Community Center.

Kaminetsky, Joseph. 2005. *Memorable Encounters.* Brooklyn, NY: The Shaar Press.

"Manny Rohan Audio Visual Testimonial." circa 1987. A project of Yale University.

"Marcus Rosenberg Audio Visual Testimonial." circa 1987. A project of the Steven Spielberg Film and Video Archive.

The Schottenstein Edition. 2001. *Babylonian Talmud, Bava Basra.* Brooklyn, New York: Mesorah Publications, Ltd.

The Stone Edition. 1996. *Tanach.* Brooklyn, New York: Mesorah Publications, Ltd.

About the Author

Courtesy of Holly Kuper Photography

lizabeth Meyer Liener, a native Dallasite, graduated Phi Beta Kappa from the University of Texas at Austin with a computer science degree. Employed by the telecommunications firm Ericsson for over sixteen years, she worked as a technical writer, programmer, and systems designer. Liener and her husband, Robert, have three children.

Made in the USA
Middletown, DE
11 November 2021

52121370R00158